PLACE-NAMES
OF THE
WIGTOWNSHIRE MOORS AND MACHARS

by

JOHN MACQUEEN

Published by
STRANRAER AND DISTRICT LOCAL HISTORY TRUST

ISBN 978 0 9542966 9 8

Published by
Stranraer and District Local History Trust
Tall Trees
London Road
Stranraer DG9 8BZ

Preface

This book extends the survey of Wigtownshire place-names begun in *Place-Names of the Rhinns of Galloway and Luce Valley* (2002). Several readers have complained that, in that book, a number of names were not discussed, or even mentioned. It would, of course, be an impossible task to discuss every individual name, even in a small area, but here I have aimed for a rather more inclusive coverage. The arrangement is historical and thematic, beginning with the oldest names and moving forward, chapter by chapter, towards the modern period. The great majority of the names are Gaelic; to these chapters 3, 4, 5 and 6 are devoted. Scottish and Irish Gaelic are both relevant. The four chapters are preceded by one on British (Welsh) names and one on Old English (Anglian) names, the first group certainly earlier than anything Gaelic, the second possibly so. The final two chapters deal with Scandinavian (Norse) names, probably from the tenth or eleventh century, and with Scottish and English names, which may have begun in the twelfth century and extend to the present. Wherever possible, I have given Ordnance Survey grid references to help with identification. There is an alphabetic index of individual names.

I have not been able to supply as many early forms as I should have liked, but hope that my selection is at least adequate. Early forms are sometimes helpful, but in Scotland, for the most part, they depend on scribes who did not know the language of the place-name, or were not literate in it; the earlier form is often no more helpful than the modern. Local pronunciation is often the best clue.

I have to thank the many people in the Machars who have been happy to share their knowledge with me while I was writing this book.

J.M.

Contents

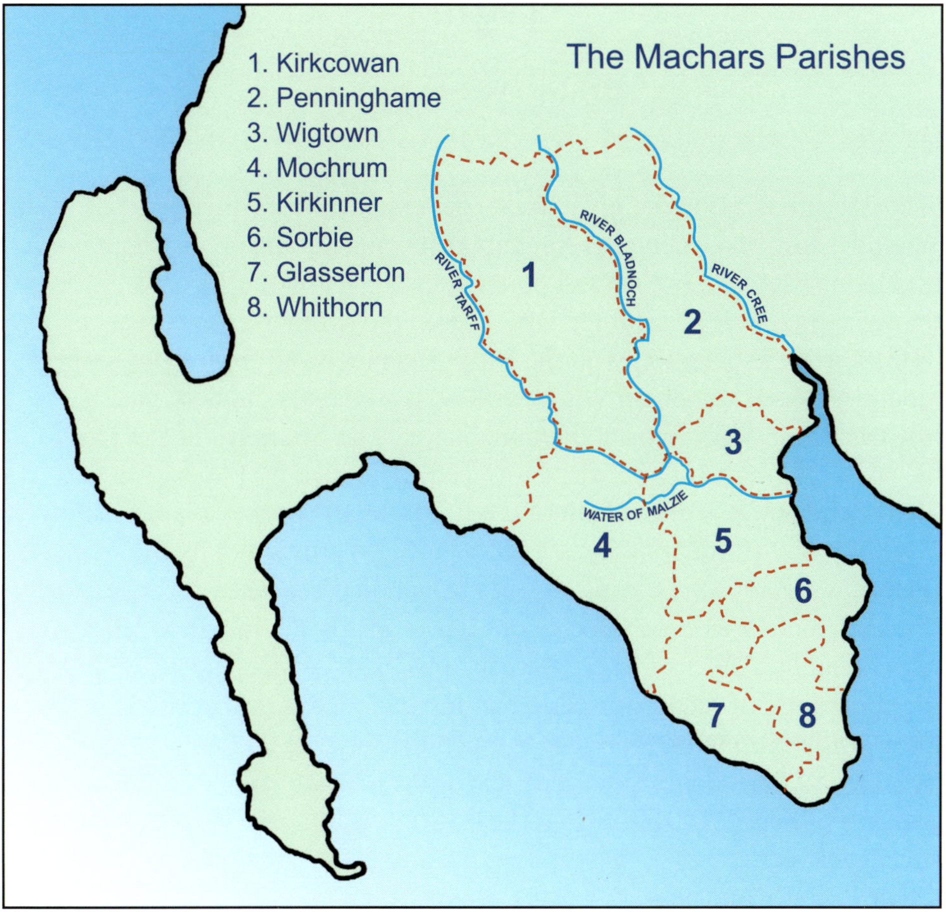
The Machars Parishes
1. Kirkcowan
2. Penninghame
3. Wigtown
4. Mochrum
5. Kirkinner
6. Sorbie
7. Glasserton
8. Whithorn
RIVER TARFF
RIVER BLADNOCH
RIVER CREE
WATER OF MALZIE
1
2
3
4
5
6
7
8

Chapter 1

British (Welsh) Names

'The **Moors**' is the name given to the generally hilly northern part of Wigtownshire, excluding the Regality of Glenluce. The precise area is usually not defined, but natural boundaries are set by the Tarf Water to the west, the River Cree to the east, and on the south the lower reaches of the Tarf to its junction with the River Bladnoch and from there to the mouth of the Bladnoch on Wigtown Bay. It covers the modern parishes of Kirkcowan, Wigtown and Penninghame. 'The **Machars**' is the area to the south, bordered on the west by Luce Bay (called by Ptolemy in the second century AD 'the mouth of the River *Abravannus*'), on the east by Wigtown Bay (Ptolemy's '*Iena* estuary'), and on the south by the Irish Sea (Ptolemy's '*Ivernian Ocean*'). As has been noted elsewhere, Abravannus, 'the extremely weak, very feeble one', is probably the Piltanton Burn rather than the Water of Luce (Breeze 2001, 151-2; MacQueen 2002, 91); the etymology of Iena is obscure, but the reference is probably to the River Cree, while Ivernian Ocean means much the same as the modern 'Irish Sea' (*Ivernia* = Ireland, Hibernia). The term Machars applies to the modern parishes of Kirkinner, Sorbie, Glasserton and Whithorn. Mochrum parish stands between the two; the northern parts at least belong to the Moors rather than the Machars.

'Moors' has an obvious English meaning. 'Machars' is the Gaelic word *machair*, 'low-lying fertile plain, extensive beach', with the addition of English plural final *-s*. Originally the term seems not to have been limited to Wigtownshire. John Maclellan, for instance, wrote a short Latin 'Description of Galloway', printed with Pont's map of Wigtownshire in Blaeu's *Atlas* (1654), where he defines Machars (*Machris*) simply as 'low-lying arable land'. He does not restrict the term to Wigtownshire.

It first appears in something like the modern sense in *A Large Description of Galloway*, written in 1684 by Andrew Symson, who was Episcopal curate of Kirkinner. Symson intended his work as a contribution to Sir Robert Sibbald's monumental *Scotia Illustrata*, which appeared in

1684, but, as it turned out, his work remained in manuscript until 1823. Symson remarks:

'The three parishes last described, viz. Sorbie, including the two annexed parishes of Kirkmadroyn [Kirkmadrine] and Crugleton [Cruggleton], Whithern and Glasserton, including the annext parish of Kirkmaiden, to which may be also added part of Kirkinner, are commonly called The Machirrs or Machirrs of Whithern, which word Machirrs, as I am informed, imports white [i.e. "fallow"] ground; and indeed those parishes contain by far much more arable and white land than up in the moors, though the parishes there be much larger.'

Essentially, that is to say, the Machars are the lands which originally formed the estates of the bishops and canons of Whithorn, a subject substantially covered in *A Monastery and its Landscape: Whithorn and Monastic Estate Management (c.1250 – c. 1600)*, the thirteenth Whithorn Lecture, delivered by Richard Oram in 2004 (Oram 2005).

There is no mention of either term in early documents. Such a lack is not uncommon in Wigtownshire place-names and complicates any study of the area. Most names were created before 1200, a time for which almost no documentary evidence exists. Certainty of interpretation is often impossible. Any study will largely depend on the analogy of more certain examples elsewhere and on simple probability.

'Moors' is derived from Old English *mor*, pl. *moras*, 'moor, waste upland, fen', and it is possible, although not perhaps particularly likely, that the name goes back as far as the Anglian period in Wigtownshire, discussed later in this chapter. In Anglo-Saxon poetry moors lie beyond the borders of society; they are the haunt of outlaws and monsters like Beowulf's opponent, Grendel. 'The grim spirit was called Grendel, a famous march-stepper, who held the moors, the fen, and the fastness' (*Beowulf*, 182-4). 'March-stepper' implies that Grendel lived on the borders, the marches, of normal existence. The Wigtownshire Moors may once have had such a connotation, long since lost.

Because 'Machars' is Gaelic, it is probably later than the Anglian period, but earlier, probably much earlier, than the sixteenth-century Reformation. The singular form *machair* is fairly common in other Wigtownshire place-names; two examples, Machermore, 242548, Old

Luce, habitation, and Macherally, 116377, Kirkmaiden, have been noted in my book on the Rhinns (MacQueen 2002, 65, 85), to which may now be added **Machermore's Mill Stone,** 392376, Glasserton, **Macher-Stewart**, 416461; Sorbie, habitation, and ***Macharsoil*** (Mochrum), the last listed by Sir Herbert Maxwell (Maxwell 1930, 206), but which I have been unable to identify. The names belong to the Machars, but refer to individual places rather than to a large area.

One other term should be mentioned, which has a church context. The organisation of the pre-Reformation diocese of Whithorn was in three rural deaneries, Rhinns, **Farines** (the remainder of Wigtownshire, i.e., Machars and Moors), and Desnes (Kirkcudbrightshire west of Urr). The etymology of Farines, like that of Desnes, is obscure.

I have already referred to the *Geography* of Ptolemy, the earliest source for place-names in Wigtownshire. There we find the name *Loucopibia* or *Loucopiabia*, which is identified as a 'city' of the *Novantae*, 'the fresh, lively, vigorous ones', the people who held Wigtownshire and perhaps the whole of Galloway during the Roman period in Britain. Almost certainly the proper form of the name should be *Leucovia.* Because the first element is Celtic **leuco-*, 'bright, shining, white', which in turn might be compared with the *candida*, 'white, shining', of Candida Casa and the 'white' of *Whit*horn, this place in the past has been identified with **Whithorn**, 442403, Whithorn, habitation. It now seems unlikely. In Ptolemy 'city' probably means either 'Roman fort' or 'hill-fort', neither applicable to Whithorn. Rivet and Smith (Rivet and Smith 1979, 389-90) make Leucovia the Roman fort at Glenlochar in Kirkcudbrightshire.

Ninian (*Nynia*) is the earliest reasonably historical figure to be associated with the Machars. Precisely how early is uncertain, but the probability is that he founded Candida Casa at **Whithorn** sometime in the fifth century AD. Bede states (*Ecclesiastical History*, III, 4) that Ninian was himself a Briton, and implies that the people around Whithorn – the descendants of the Novantae – were also Britons; his church was built of stone 'in a manner to which the Britons were not accustomed'. The language of these people was an early cognate of Welsh.

The existence of early churches in such Welsh-speaking areas is often indicated by place-names in **egles*, a term derived from Latin, ultimately Greek, *ecclesia* (ἐκκλησία), 'church'. In modern place-names the word usually appears as 'Eccles'. Examples are to be found in the Rhinns and Luce Valley (MacQueen 2002, 95-6; 2005, 134-6), but, curiously enough, none in the Moors and Machars.

Bede also makes it clear that by the early eighth century political and religious control had passed into the hands of the Northumbrian Angles who spoke a northern dialect of Anglo-Saxon or Old English. Their political control had perhaps been established in the middle-seventh century, while full ecclesiastic control was marked by the appointment of Bede's friend Pecthelm as bishop of Whithorn, shortly before the completion of the *Ecclesiastical History* in 731. A sequence of Anglo-Saxon bishops continued at least into the early-ninth century and probably longer.

The main linguistic sequence to the ninth century – Welsh/British succeeded and to some degree replaced, by the Anglian of Northumbria – is thus tolerably clear. Both Welsh and the Anglian form of Old English have left traces in the place-names. Welsh names tend to occur in the Moors rather than the Machars, a feature which suggests that in the south, closer to Whithorn, Anglian became predominant.

The names of the two streams, reaches of which mark the division between Machars and Moors, were both given by the Britons at an early (pre-Christian) date. Both have mythological overtones. **Tarf** is derived from the Celtic root **taruo-*, Welsh *tarw*, 'bull'; the reference is to the river as an agent of fecundity, fertility. **Bladnoch** is derived from the root **blato-*, Welsh *blawd*, 'flower', 'flour', probably also 'corn', combined with the feminine suffix *-ona*, signifying divinity, the supernatural. Compare Gaulish *Matrona*, the river Marne, regarded as a mother goddess. The Bladnoch was a lesser divinity than the Marne; the final syllable, *-och*, is the diminutive, earlier British *-acca*. The original form would thus have been **Blatonacca*, 'little female corn-divinity'. The junction of the male Tarf, 'bull', with the female Bladnoch at **The Holm**, 347602, Kirkcowan, habitation, ensured the fertility of the surrounding land; compare the junction of another bull, the Tarff Water, with the Dee (*deva*, 'goddess') below Tongland Bridge, 690532, in the Stewartry.

The root *blato-* occurs elsewhere; compare *Blatobulgium*, 'flour-

Junction of Tarf ('bull') and Bladnoch — 'little corn-goddess'

Ochiltree, 'high fermtoun'

sack', the name given in the *Antonine Itinerary* to the Roman fort at Birrens, Dumfriesshire, and *Blatomagus*, 'flowery field', now Blond, Haut-Vienne, France. Compare also *Bladon* in Oxfordshire, where the name of the village has been taken from the old name of the neighbouring stream, now the Evenlode.

High, **Middle** and **Low Threave,** 375594, 369588, 376585, Wigtown, habitations, are farms above the left bank of the Bladnoch, below its confluence with the Tarf. **Threave Hill**, 368587, 63 m., and **Low Threave Moss** are nearby. The triple division is late, the result of the Agricultural Revolution of the eighteenth century. On his map of Wigtownshire in Blaeu's *Atlas*, Timothy Pont marks only a single settlement, *Treef*. High and Low Threave are marked as separate on Ainslie's map 0f 1782; Middle Threave marks a still later division.

Ochiltree, 324743, Penninghame, habitation, is further north, close to the Carrick border. Nearby is **Hill of Ochiltree**, 326741, 184 m., and **Loch Ochiltree**. On Pont's map the form is *Vchiltry*.

Ochiltree is a compound of two common Welsh words, *uchel*, 'high', and *tref*, *tre*, 'homestead, house (and surrounding land), farm, estate' (*GPC*). The name corresponds to the geographical position; the farm stands at a height of 125 metres. There is another Scottish Ochiltree in Ayrshire and a third in West Lothian. In Wales, *Ucheldre* occurs in Anglesey, Caernarvon, Montgomery, Cardigan and Radnor; twice in Merioneth.

Threave is simply *tref*, 'homestead', with no qualifying adjective. In Kirkcudbrightshire the same name is attached to the castle of the Douglases on an island in the River Dee. In Wales there are no instances of unsupported *Tref* as a place-name, but it does once occur as Dref in Herefordshire, on the Welsh border.

The modern form **Monreith**, 361408; Mochrum, habitation, would seem to suggest that the first element is the Scottish Gaelic *mon* or *monadh*, itself an adaptation of the earlier Welsh or Pictish word *mynydd*, 'hill, mountain' (see discussion below). Earlier forms however suggest a different etymology. A charter dated 15 January 1481 has *quartam partem terrarum et baronie de Mureith*, 'the fourth part of the lands and barony of *Mureith*' (*RMS* ii, 1499). Maxwell quotes another form, *Murrief*, but gives no source. The stress pattern offers some difficulty, but these forms at least suggests a parallel with early records of the name of the province of Moray, *Murebe* (*Annals of Ulster*, 1032), *Muireb* (*AU*, 1085) *Moreb* (*AU*, 1130), records indicating a partly-Gaelicised compound of Welsh *môr* (Gaelic *muir*), 'sea' and *tref.* Monreith, in other words, may well be a compound with *tref* as the second element, meaning 'homestead, fermtoun, by the sea'. Topography supports the etymology. **Monreith Bay** takes its name from the modern hamlet.

Tref-, followed by a defining noun or adjective, is reasonably common in Scottish place-names. Examples are *Ter*regles, 'church-farm', in Kirkcudbrightshire, *Tra*prain, 'steading of the tree', in East Lothian, and *Tra*quair, 'farm on the River Quair', in Peeblesshire. Similar names are widespread in Wales, Cornwall and Brittany. They are also found in parts of England; in Cumberland *Tri*ermain (= *tref yr maen*, 'homestead of the stone'), in Lancashire *Trea*les (= *treflys*, 'court-village'), and in Herefordshire *Tre*gate (= *tregoed*, 'hamlet of the wood'). In all these, it will be noticed, the qualifying element follows *tref.* The form of the names, that is to say, is neo-Celtic probably no earlier than the sixth century AD. **Ochiltree** and **Monreith**, with the qualifying adjective or noun preceding and compounded with the defining final noun, follows an earlier linguistic pattern, found in many names in the British section of Ptolemy's *Geography* and on the continent in Roman Gaul, Spain and Italy. Compare *Uxelodunum*, 'high fort', which in Roman times was found in Cumbria (the fort at Stanwix on the River Eden near Carlisle) and on the Continent (e.g., modern *Issoudun*, Indre, France). *Uxelo-* is an ancestral form of Welsh *uchel*; *dunum*, 'fort' becomes Welsh *din*, Gaelic *dun*, 'fort'. *Moridunum*, 'fort by the sea', was the early name for what is now Carmarthen in Wales. The names Ochiltree and Monreith may thus have been in existence even before Ninian's time.

Threave, a name made up of a single element, may also be early. Equally it may reflect local usage. In conversation, a phrase like 'the town' means whatever town is nearest, be it Stranraer, Glasgow, Birmingham or London. So with a phrase like 'the farm' in a farming neighbourhood – the nearest farm is usually to be understood. Threave may once have had a longer name, now vanished. What has survived is the immediately local usage.

During the Roman period, place-names in *tref*, or rather the root **trebo*-, seem relatively rare. Curiously enough, most are to be found in Spain, where we have the place *Contrebia* in the province of Guadalajara and the tribe *Arrotrebae* somewhere in the north. There are several other instances. One British example, *Locatrebe*, meaning 'lake-village' or 'pool-dwellers', possibly with reference to a crannog, appears to have been in Scotland south of the Antonine Wall, probably in the south-west. The site must have resembled that of the Wigtownshire Ochiltree. The name *Atrebates*, which gives its name to the modern *Arras*, Pas de Calais, France, was originally that of a people in northern France with a branch in southern Britain. The remains of *Calleva Atrebatum*, 'Calleva of the Atrebates', are near the modern Silchester, Hampshire. Atrebates is formed from the root *trebo*- with the prefix *ad*- and the verbal-adjectival suffix *–tis* (plural *–tes*)., and means simply 'settlers, inhabitants'; compare Welsh *athref*, 'abode' and the Irish verbal-noun *attrab*, 'act of inhabiting, dwelling in'. As with Threave, there was no need, at least locally, to be more specific.

The absence from the record of other early names involving the same root need not cause surprise. The Atrebates were politically important. Most modern *tref*-names however involve places unlikely to be mentioned in historic documents, at least of the kind that have come down to us from classical antiquity. It is entirely possible that names in **trebo*- were once as common as modern names in -*tref*-, but remained unrecorded, and have since completely disappeared, perhaps replaced by names from an incoming different language.

Names in -*tref*- reflect one important aspect of the society which produced them. I quote A.H. Williams (Williams 1949, 134):

'The tref or hamlet was the clan or subdivision of a clan organized as an economic unit. Wales during the Dark Ages was predominantly a pastoral country, with a little agriculture carried on here and there. The rearing of cattle, sheep, and swine was therefore the main occupation of the people, though a certain amount of oats, barley, and, more rarely, wheat was grown. The forests provided firewood and building material, as well as bees and their honey; freemen could hunt, hawk, and fish; while clothing was made at home. Each clan was therefore more or less self-sufficing, though there was naturally a certain amount of division of labour. The only specialized calling of note was that of the smith, important because it furnished the warriors with their weapons.'

Each *tref* of this kind formed part of a *cantref*, 'cantred, hundred'; in round figures one hundred *tref*s grouped together for administrative and judicial functions. Treales, 'court-village' in Lancashire, was once probably the centre of legal procedures for such a cantref. To quote Williams again (p.141), 'The scope of the cantref courts was very wide indeed. They could decide disputes as to the rightful ownership of land; they could listen to claims for temporary possession of land under the process known as *dadanhudd*; and they could determine disputable boundaries, for the Welsh at that time, as in later years, were guilty of encroaching on one another's territory – "The digging up of boundary ditches, the removal of landmarks, the outstripping of bounds, the occupation and extension of lands by hook or by crook are a passion with this people beyond any other race." So wrote Giraldus Cambrensis, a most acute observer in the twelfth century.'

The ruler of the cantref was chief of the extended clan, in early times probably styled 'king', but later usually 'lord'. One of his tasks was the administration of justice, but the primary one was the defence and extension of his territory and people. First and foremost, he was a warrior.

The situation may be illustrated by the name Traprain Law, East Lothian. Traprain is a compound of *tref* and *pren*, 'tree', 'tref of the tree', but the name is now restricted to a single notable crag on which a fortified tribal capital stood during the Roman and sub-Roman period. From twelfth-century documents we know that the original name was *Dunpelder*, Welsh *din*, 'fort' and *pelydr*, plural of *paladr*, 'spear-shaft', 'fort of spearshafts'. Traprain, we may deduce, was the name of the *tref* in which the fort stood and, to judge by its name and other evidence, the inhabitants of the fort were warriors. The lord of the fort must have been responsible for more than a single *tref*; the documents present him as in fact a king, Leudonus, eponym of Lothian, over which presumably he reigned from Traprain Law. Several other *-tref*-names have survived in the area; *Tra*nent, *Tra*broun, Longnid*dry* in East Lothian; *Tor*quhan, Nid*drie* and Sou*tra* in Midlothian; Nid*dry* and Ochil*tree* in West Lothian. As a whole however Lothian is too big to have formed a single *cantref* – there were seven in the Welsh kingdom of Dyfed, the modern Pembrokeshire together with the western part of Carmarthen. Lothian must have had at least three, with a second major fortified site on Edinburgh Castle Rock and conceivably another in West Lothian. The general situation however is clear. One of the king's major fortresses was in the *tref* of Traprain.

In the Machars **Cruggleton Castle** (475429; Sorbie) may have performed a similar function. As is shown immediately below, the name is partly Welsh and the site is of great natural strength. 'Excavation at the ditched promontory fortification of Cruggleton have shown that it too entered a stone-built phase in the later thirteenth century, probably at the hands of John Comyn, earl of Buchan ... the occupation of the site, though, goes back to the late Iron Age' (Geoffrey Stell, 'Medieval Buildings and Secular Lordship' in Oram and Stell 1991, 148). Threave in Kirkcudbrightshire probably has a similar history.

Modern **Wigtown**, 432555; Wigtown, habitation, is also a possible site for the capital of the cantref. If so, however, no trace remains of the name by which it was known in earlier times.

It is not unreasonable to suppose that the Moors and Machars once formed a cantref, of which Threave, Ochiltree and Monreith offer the only remaining linguistic traces. The cantref may also have been a kingdom. Ailred of Rievaulx in the first chapter of his twelfth-century *Life of Ninian* thinks that the saint belonged to the area round Whithorn and that his father was a king. He also mentions (chapter 4) another king, Tudwal, ruling in the same area, and observes that 'the whole island [of Britain] was divided and subject to various kings' – to provincial and tribal kings on the Irish pattern, that is to say. As it stands, the evidence is late, but it may be based on earlier documentary material as well as tradition. It fits the general picture of sub-Roman Britain as it has come down to us.

Ochiltree, Threave and Monreith are important, partly because they are unmistakeably Welsh, but still more for the evidence they provide on the early structure of local society. It is perhaps worth noting that this structure was not confined to the more fertile Machars. The first two names belong to the Moors. Ochiltree in particular is well away from the Machars. Whether or not the two areas once formed a single cantref, almost certainly both shared a common system of land division and management. Later names in Anglian *-ton*, Gaelic *Auch-* and *Bal-*, or Scandinavian *–by* may sometimes have obliterated older names in *tref-*.

A good map of *-tref-* names in Scotland will be found in Nicolaisen 1976,167. Curiously, Threave is excluded, as is Monreith. Accompanying the map is a discussion of the names. A slightly less useful map and discussion, also by Nicolaisen, will be found in McNeill and MacQueen 1996, 50-51.

Geoffrey Barrow (Barrow 1973, 7-68) has written interestingly on the pre-history of the system of shires and thanes in pre-feudal Scotland and England, a system which he suspects is ultimately British or Welsh, a system, that is to say, based on the cantref. As indicators he singles out the words **egles* (Eccles, etc.), 'church', and *caer*, 'fort' (in Latin records often represented by *urbs*) as likely to be particularly important. I do not question this judgement, merely suggesting that *-tref-* is equally, even perhaps more, important. The distribution map confirms some of Barrow's proposals, but also extends them into districts which he leaves uncovered – Galloway and south Ayrshire, for instance, also Buchan, and the Moray Firth coastline.

Half-a-mile south-west of Middle Threave, above the Bladnoch, is **Pauples Hill**, 360583, Penninghame, 47 m., Welsh *pabell*, 'tent, temporary dwelling, booth', with English plural *-s*. The meaning is 'hill of the tents or booths'. The people of the *tref* practised transhumance, a system by which in early summer they drove their animals to pastures on higher, uncultivated ground, thus allowing crops to ripen undisturbed. The women and children who tended the herds lived in the tents or booths. Compare *Pibble* and *Pibble Hill* in Kirkmabreck parish, Kirkcudbright; also the town of *Peebles*. *Pabell* corresponds in meaning to Gaelic *airidh*, 'shieling', on which see MacQueen 2002, 38-41; also below, pp.. The word is derived from Latin *papilio*, usually 'butterfly', but with a derived meaning, 'tent, pavilion'. It seems likely that Roman legionaries on the march referred jokingly to their tents as 'butterflies' and that the word in this sense was adopted by the subject Britons.

In Welsh the basic sense of the word *tor* is 'belly'. This is extended to mean 'flank, side (of a hill)', (river) bank'. In this sense it is a common element in Welsh place-names, found also in the Wigtownshire

Cruggleton ('hill — hill-fermtoun') Castle

Torhouse (**The Standing Stones of Torhouse,** 382565; Wigtown, **Mains of Torhouse,** 384550, habitation; **Little Torhouse**, 389563, habitation; **Torhousekie Farm**, 377568, habitation; **Torhousemuir House**, 394568, habitation; and **Torhouse Mill**, 398552, habitation. **Torhouse Rocks** are on the right bank of the Bladnoch, opposite Torhouse Mill). The name is hybrid, with the first element Welsh *tor*, and the second English or Scandinavian *hus*, 'house' (*hus* 'is mainly found in Scandinavian England' *ODEPN*, s.v.). The meaning is 'house on the side of a hill', or 'on a river bank'. The names are spread over a fairly wide area, but *Tor*- probably originally referred to the **Bladnoch**; in particular, **The Standing Stones of Torhouse** stand on the hilly left bank, and the original 'house' may well have been these Standing Stones. **Torhousekie** appears as *Toreous-Makkee*, and as *Torhous Makke* (*RMS* iii, 1951, 2353; 22 December 1570, 26 January 1575; in the latter it is sold *Joanni Makculloch de Torhous*). Pont has *Torhowse MacKulloch* (a place marked as being of some importance), *Torhouse Macky* and *Torhowse Moore*. John McCulloch, who purchased Torhousekie, presumably lived at *Torhouse McCulloch*, on the site of the modern **Torhousemuir House**, where the older name has been abandoned in favour of *Torhowse Moore*.

The first element in **Cruggleton,** 480432, Sorbie, habitation, is Welsh *crug*, 'hillock, knoll', also found in some Romano-British names, ***Cro**cocolana*, the Roman settlement at Brough, Nottinghamshire, and *Penno**cruc**ium*, now represented by the village of *Pen**krid**ge*, Staffordshire, although the original site is at Water Eaton, some 2 ½ miles away to the south. The second element, *-le-*, belongs to a different language; it is Old English *hyll*, 'hill', with a meaning similar to that of *crug*. The final element, *-ton*, indicates the fermtoun which grew up round the site, now represented by **Cruggleton Castle**, and itself originally perhaps a *tref.* Compare Crudgington, Shropshire, for which a form *Crugelton* exists in records from the twelfth century, and Crigglestone, Yorkshire, where the *-s-* is intrusive. The names mean 'hillock-hill-fermtoun'. Such tautological place-names are common when one language is replacing another; cf. the discussion of Nick of the Balloch and Gabsnout in MacQueen 2002, 17, 21.

In Wales *crug* appears by itself and also as the first element in compound place-names. In Cruggleton it may originally have figured simply as *crug* or it may have formed part of a longer name – no certainty can be reached. Anglian settlers regarded it as the name of a hill and adapted it accordingly.

A similar tautological hybrid is **Pen Hill**, 409474; Sorbie, 68 m., where the first element, perhaps Welsh *pen*, 'head, headland, promontory, projecting piece of rock', is combined with English 'hill', of much the same meaning. See, however, below, chapter 3. Despite appearances, **Penticle,** 415512; Kirkinner, is different; it is a variant spelling of Scots *pendicle*, 'a small piece of ground forming part of a larger holding or farm and frequently let to a sub-tenant … Often applied as a place-name to small pieces of ground, originally *pendicles* but now detached and independent' (*SND*). It is an adaptation of medieval Latin *pendiculum*, a noun formed from Latin *pendere*, 'to hang', with the diminutive suffix *–iculum*, literally 'a small hanger-on'.

W.J. Watson (Watson 1926, 180) linked **Drumwalt,** 308538, Mochrum, habitation, with Leswalt, 018639, Leswalt, habitation, in the Rhinns, and in both interpreted *–walt* as Welsh *gwellt*, 'grass'. Drumwalt would then be 'grassy ridge', with Welsh *trum*, 'mountain, hill, peak, ridge', cognate with Gaelic *druim*, as the first element. In MacQueen 2002, 93, I cast some doubt on this etymology of Leswalt, doubts which also apply to Drumwalt.

A number of Welsh streams are called *Caletwr* or *Cletwr*, a compound of the adjective *caled*, 'hard', and *dwr* or *dwfr*. The name goes back to an earlier British **caletodubron*, 'hard water'. Outside Wales, the usual form is *Calder*, which occurs as the name of streams in Cumberland, Lancashire, and the West Riding of Yorkshire. There are many Calders in Scotland, where the name also appears as Cawdor and Callander (Watson 1926, 105-6, 197, 455-6, 522). The one Wigtownshire example is **Calder Loch**, 277730; Kirkcowan, formed by an unnamed tributary of the **Polbae Burn** just above its confluence with the Bladnoch at 278728.

A Gaelicized form of *dwr* or *dwfr*, appears in **Dourie** and **North Dourie Cottage**, 346434, 347440; Mochrum, habitations. Dourie is *dobhrág*, a Gaelic adaptation of *dwfr*, with added feminine diminutive suffix *-ág*, 'little water or stream' (Watson 1926, 456). The stream reference is not clear, perhaps to some burn which has disappeared as a consequence of modern field-drainage techniques.

Watson devoted his chapter xii to what he called 'British-Gaelic Names', names, that is to say, based on an element originally British, not found in the Gaelic of Ireland, but at some point incorporated into the vocabulary of Scottish Gaelic. His first example is the word *monadh*, 'hill-ground', which he regarded as a Gaelic adaptation of 'Welsh *mynydd*, older *minit*, a mountain, from an earlier *monijo-*; --- In modern Gaelic *monadh* means hill ground, hilly region: in Perthshire it is *mon*, and this short form was apparently used elsewhere in districts which are not now Gaelic-speaking' (p.391). The best-known surviving instance of the word as a place-name is 'The Mounth', the great ridge which divides Scotland north of Forth in two – the 'steep and rugged mountains' which, according to Bede, separated the Northern from the Southern Picts.

There are many others. At least one Galloway example is pure Welsh: Minnigaff, 411664, Minnigaff, habitation, in Kirkcudbrightshire, just across the Cree from Penninghame parish, is on record (*RMS* iv, 218, 23 June 1548) as *Monygof*, i.e., *mynydd y gof*, 'hill-ground of the smith', with the first element *monadh* or *mon*. Several hill-names in the Moors, and one in the Machars, contain the same element: in Kirkcowan parish, **Big** and **Wee Munrogie,** 274742, 277740, 155 and 150 m., **Monjorie**, 268735, 157 m., **Minnigie**, 270734, 152 m., **Monandie** (with stress on the second syllable) **Rig,** 243704, 192 m., **High** and **Low Mindork**, 308585, 315590, habitations, near **Mindork Fell**, 321584, 94 m., together with **Knockmononday**, 368567, Penninghame, 37 m., and **Minicarlie**, 391386; Glasserton, 90 m. This last is a short distance to the north of **Carleton**, 392379; Glasserton**,** habitation**,** the source of the second, defining element *–carlie*. The meaning is 'hill-ground close or belonging to Carleton'. In at least some of the others the defining element is Gaelic. **Monjorie**, for instance, has the second element *deòradh*, 'stranger, outlaw, exile', but also 'custodian of the relic of a saint'; compare High Glenjorrie, 208584, Old Luce, habitation. The two names may originally both have referred to the same 'dewar', the hereditary keeper of a reliquary. In **Minniegie** the second element is *gaoithe*, genitive singular of *gaoth*, 'wind', 'windy hill'.

On Pont's map **Monandie Rig** is simply *Monenduy*, apparently a fermetoun. It is *mon na h-annaide*, 'hill-ground of the annat'; compare

Cairnhandy, 091453, Stoneykirk, habitation. **Knockmononday** is tautological, 'hill of the hill-ground of the annat'. For this last term, see below, chapter 3, pp..

Mindork (*RMS* iii, 2521, 14 February 1500, *Mondork*; 3294, 29 January 1508, *Mundork*) is *mon na d-torc*, 'hill-ground of the boars', with eclipsis of initial *t* by *d-* after the genitive plural *na* of the definite article, a usage which has disappeared in modern Scottish Gaelic, although it survives in Irish.

I have no more than a tentative explanation of the *–rogie* in Munrogie. The first part may be the intensive prefix *ro-*, the second *gáeth*, genitive plural of Old Irish *gáeth* (Gaelic *gaoth*), 'hill-ground of the strong winds'.

Watson has also demonstrated (Watson 1926, 414) that a word commonly used in Welsh place-names, *dol*, 'meadow, dale, valley', was adapted into Scots Gaelic as *dail-*, usually represented in Scots as *Dal-*, with the same meaning as in the Welsh. Dalkeith (Midlothian) is entirely Welsh, *dol* + *coed*, 'wood', 'valley of the wood, wooded valley'. Dalmarnock in the east end of Glasgow shows the adapted form *dail-* + *mo Ernog*, 'my little Ernáin', the distinctively Gaelic pet-name of a probably Irish saint.

Three Wigtownshire examples – Dalkest, 022695, Kirkcolm, Dalminnoch, 082644, Inch, habitation, and Dalnigap, 133710, New Luce, habitation – were discussed in my book on the Rhinns and Glenluce, but in the Moors and Machars, to the best of my knowledge, there is only one doubtful example, **Dalreagle,** 374553, Kirkinner, a farm-name, also found in the nearby **Dalreagle Cottage**, 368550, habitation, **Dalreagle Ford** (across the Bladnoch), 372557, and **Dalreagle Steps,** 370557, on **Wood Hill**, 368557, 52 m. Maxwell notes that the name is pronounced *Dareagle*, with stress on the second syllable, and offers an impossible etymology, Gaelic *deargail*, 'a spot of red or cultivated land'. He does not record the earlier forms, *Dyreygill* on Pont's map, and *Dereagill* (*RPC*, 3, series x, 264). In Middle Scots *l* is 'transformed or elided in punctuation (and sometimes in spelling), though present in etymology … after *a*' (Gregory Smith 1902, xxiv). This might explain the pronunciation, but scarcely the early spellings. The first element in Dalreagle may not be *dail-*, but instead

Gaelic *doire*, 'oak-grove, thicket' (MacQueen 2002, 68). In either case, the second element is Gaelic *riaghail*, 'rule', sometimes found as a stream-name, for instance the Regal Burn in Avondale, Lanarkshire. In Watson's discussion of the word (Watson 1926, 147-8), he mentions ***Carsregale***, mentioned, together with Urrall, Kilquhockadale, and the unidentified ***Arenemord*** (all Kirkcowan), in a charter dated 13 November 1546 (*RMS* iv, 30). It is now probably **Carseriggan** (316677; Kirkcowan). The name looks like an inversion compound, with first element Scots *carse*, 'the stretch of low alluvial land along the banks of some Scottish rivers' (*OED*), and the second *riaghail*, probably the name, now lost, of a burn in the neighbourhood. The **Black Burn**, a tributary of the Bladnoch, is the main possibility. In **Dalreagle** the reference must be to the Bladnoch itself.

Watson comments that 'The special meaning of *riaghail* in names of places is not clear to me'. I suggest that sometimes at least it may indicate a boundary. Another possibility is that it may refer to a religious rule, like that of St Benedict. The place or stream may have belonged to a monastic community.

Culbratten, 388628; Penninghame, habitation, is a Gaelic name, but one which indicates the survival of Welsh-speakers in a Gaelic-speaking milieu. It is *cùil nam Breatann*, 'nook, corner, of the Britons, where Britons live'. Compare Drumbreddan, 083440, Stoneykirk, habitation: *druim nam Breatann*, 'ridge of the Britons', which also bears witness to the survival of British-speakers (MacQueen 2002, 91). The first element in **Bratney Walls Pond**, 399509; Kirkinner, is Gaelic *Breatnach*, 'Briton, Welshman' and may originally have referred to a Welsh-speaker. Alternatively, it may be a shortened form of the surname McBretney, which itself means 'son, descendant of a Welshman'.

Whithorn, Candida Casa — 'white hut'

Chapter 2

Old English (Anglian) Names

The period of Anglian supremacy in the Rhinns is best documented in terms of the church at **Whithorn**. The actual supremacy may have begun in the time of Oswiu, king of Northumbria 655-70, but the first event to be recorded is the election, c.730, of Pecthelm as bishop of Whithorn. In 735 he was succeeded by Frithewald, who in turn was succeeded by Pectwine in 763. In 776 or 777 Æthelberht was consecrated as bishop at York. In 789 he was translated to Hexham and in 791 he assisted at the consecration of Beadwulf, his successor at Whithorn. In 803 Beadwulf was still in office. A bishop Heathored is recorded in the middle 830s. The language of all these names is Old English.

In the later eighth century a Latin poem, the *Miracles of Bishop Nynia* (Ninian), was composed at Whithorn (MacQueen 2005, 88-101). In this are preserved the Anglian names of two men with links to the church, Pethgils, a layman who became a monk, and a priest Plecgils. Two others, a man and a woman mentioned but not named in the *Miracles*, are recorded in the much later *Life of Ninian* by Ailred of Rievaulx (1110-67) as Adelfrid and Deisuit. All four lived in the eighth century and their names are again Old English.

Several of these names appear to preserve the element *Pect-*, 'Pict'.

In or about 840 the church was destroyed by fire, perhaps in the course of the fatal raid on Galloway made by Alpin (MacQueen 2002, 13-14). The building was soon replaced (Hill 1997, 20, 162-4). In the early 880s refugees from Viking assaults on Lindisfarne brought the relics of their former bishop, St Cuthbert, briefly to Whithorn.

Whithorn remained under the metropolitan authority of the archbishops of York until 1355. It was placed under the metropolitan authority of St Andrews in 1472 and transferred to the province of Glasgow in 1492 (Watt 1969, 128).

More information is to be found in the Old English place-names of the region. **Whithorn** (442403; Whithorn), rendering the earlier Latin

Candida Casa, is unique in having reasonably early documentation. Elsewhere (MacQueen 2005, 16-21) I have pointed out that *casa* in Candida Casa means 'cabin' or 'hut', not 'house'. This was recognised by the late-ninth-century translator of Bede, who rendered [*Ad*] *Candidam Casam* by [*æt þæm*] *Hwitan Ærne,* '[at the] white *ærn*'. *Hwiterne* is the form found under the year 565 in the Laud MS of the *Anglo-Saxon Chronicle*, a MS the greater part of which was transcribed from earlier sources at Peterborough, probably in 1121. In English place-names *ærn* generally means 'storehouse, shed'; compare such names as Colerne (Wilts.), 'shed where charcoal was stored', Cowarne (Hereford), 'cowshed, byre', Hardhorn (Lancs.), 'storehouse' (O.E. *hordern*). Latin *casa* and OE *ærn* both reflect the deliberately humble style of building adopted by Ninian in his original monastic foundation. The adjective 'white' conveys the idea of purity, chastity, redemption. Literally the name means 'white shed', figuratively, 'shed of redemption'.

The Latin *Life* of the Irish St Tigernach of Clones, co. Monaghan, gives, as an alternative name, ***Alba***, 'white' (Heist 1965, 108). This is the adjective used in the Gospels of Matthew (17:2) and Luke (9:29) when the garments of Jesus at the Transfiguration become white as snow: *vestimenta autem eius facta sunt* ***alba*** *sicut nix*. It is also applied to the redeemed in Revelation 7:9; they are *amicti stolas* ***albas***, 'dressed in white garments'. So in Psalm 50:9, addressed, it was believed, to God by King David in repentance for his murderous seduction of Bathsheba: *Lavabis me et super nivem de*_**alba**_*bor*, 'You will wash me and I shall become whiter than snow'.

Other early names for Whithorn are ***Rosnat*** (Gaelic *ros*, 'wood, promontory' with diminutive suffix *–nat*), 'little wood' or 'little promontory', and the Latin ***Magnum Monasterium***, 'big, great monastery', which is perhaps to be compared with *Maior Monasterium*, 'greater monastery', the name of the hermitage founded by St Martin near Tours in France, modern Marmoutier. This last clearly reflects the monastery at a later, grander, stage of development, perhaps the Northumbrian minster postulated by Peter Hill (Hill 1997, 40-48).

Wigtown, 432555; Wigtown, habitation, should probably be considered in association with Wigg, near Whithorn, a name now preserved

Wigtown, 'hill with a dairy-farm on it'

in **Castlewigg** and **Broadwigg**, 429432, 435436, Whithorn, habitations. The castle of Castlewigg is the ruined tower. In the strange charter by which Robert, lay commendator of Whithorn makes over the lands of the priory to the deceased Regent Moray, his heirs and assignees (*RMS* iv, 2823, 1 January 1579) we have *Meikle-Wige* and *Myd-Wyge*; on Pont's map *N*[orth]. *Wÿg*, *M*[id]. *Wÿg* (with castle), and *O*[uter]. *Wÿg*. *Wigg* and the first element in *Wig*town are probably both derived from OE *wic*, an early borrowing of Latin *vicus*, 'row of houses, quarter (of a city), street, village, hamlet, country-seat'. Wigg represents the simplex *wic*, found as Wick, the name of a number of places in south-west England. The final -*g* is probably due to Gaelic influence; compare The Wig (Kirkcolm) from ON *vík*, 'bay', and note the contrast of Wick in a non-Gaelic-speaking area of Caithness, with Uig in Gaelic-speaking Skye, both names also derived from *vík*.

The situation of the modern burgh of Wigtown suggests that the name is a compound of *wic* and OE *dun*, 'down, hill', 'hill with a *wic* on it', 'hill of the *wic*'; compare Wigton (Yorks., W Riding) with the same etymology. A less likely derivation is provided by the comparison with Wigton (Cumberland), which seems to contain the OE personal name *Wicga* combined with *tun*, 'Wicga's farm'. Less likely too is the derivation from *wic-tun*, 'dwelling-place, homestead, manor', which I suggested in MacQueen 2002, 16-17.

If the proposed etymologies are correct, both Wigg and Wigtown stand formally well apart from other Scottish place-names in *wic*, in all of which the word forms the second element of a compound name and refers to some kind of fermtoun. Berwick in North Berwick (E. Lothian) and Berwick (Northumberland), for instance, are both derived from *berewic*, 'barley farm'. Other examples are Borthwick (Midlothian), Hawick (Roxburgh) and Prestwick (Ayrshire). Arguably, the names found in Wigtownshire belong to an older stratum.

During the Roman Empire, *vicus* had 'both a colloquial and a technical meaning. Colloquially it means any village or insignificant town. Technically it means a town which, though possessing some administrative organisation of its own, is yet subordinate to a higher authority, whether civil (a *civitas*) or military (as in the case of *vici* attached to forts) or the administrator (*procurator*) of an imperial estate; in this technical sense it was applied to the internal wards of large cities' (Rivet and Smith 1979, xviii). The Anglo-Saxon invaders of Roman Britain appear to have adopted the word first in something like the technical sense – 'It would thus seem that a group of houses and associated structures, generally sited on a still usable Roman road, might be recognized here and there by early Anglo-Saxons as being, or having once been, a *vicus*' (Myres 1986, 35). Later they seem to have applied it particularly to farms, in particular dairy-farms and, in one area at least, to salt-works.

In this context it may be significant that Peter Hill's excavations at Whithorn have uncovered the remains of what seems to be a Roman road, 'a broad roadway traversing the excavated area, which must have been earlier than the late-fifth century, but cannot be dated with greater precision. The road might have led from the Isle of Whithorn to a fourth or fifth century church or settlement at the east end of the hill' (Hill 1997, 26). The presence of this road indicates the possibility that the settlement at Whithorn was once classified as a *vicus* or that incoming Anglo-Saxons regarded it as once having been a *vicus*. Wigg is close to the site of an early bishop's residence and it is at least suggestive that Wigtown later became home to the sheriff of the area.

The most probable meaning of Wigg, however, must remain 'dairy-farm', of Wigtown 'hill with a dairy-farm on it'. Possibly there remained some trace of *vicus* in the technical sense.

The second element, *-berrick*, of **Landberrick,** 363455, Mochrum, habitation (Pont's *Lamberisk* is corrupt) is probably a compound of OE *wic* already mentioned, *berewic*, literally 'barley-farm', but generally meaning 'grange, the outlying part of an estate'. Compare Berrick Prior and Salome, Oxfordshire and the pronunciation of the names Berwick (Northumberland) and North Berwick (E. Lothian). *Land-* probably indicates that the grange was inland rather than on the coast; compare Landbeach and Waterbeach (Cambridgeshire), where the names indicate relative proximity to the River Ouse. Landberrick lies well inland, close to the boundaries separating Mochrum, Kirkinner and Glasserton parishes or, from another point of view, separating the baronies of Mochrum, Glasserton and Longcastle. The meaning would thus be 'inland grange on the outlying part of Whithorn land'. I have found no early forms.

Long Castle

There may once have been a Waterberrick or Seaberrick; cf. **Killantrae** (Mochrum) below, chapter 3, pp..

A group of names in the neighbourhood of Whithorn, may also preserve *-wic* with the loss of initial *w-*. In a charter dated 18 October 1576 (*RMS* iv, 2593) **Ers*ock*** in **High Ers*ock***, 441376, Glasserton, habitation, and **Low Ers*ock***, 447377, Whithorn, habitation, appears as *Ovir* and *Nethir Ersik*. The great charter already mentioned (*ibid*., 2823, 1 January 1579) has *molendinam de Arsik cum terris molendinariis*, 'the mill of *Arsik* with the mill lands'. The mill was on the **Ersock Burn**, probably at Low Ersock. The name probably consists of an unidentified Anglo-Saxon personal name together with *–wic*, '*E*'s fermtoun'.

Stann*ock* and **Stann*ock* Cottages**, 474376, 477373, Whithorn, habitations, are found as *Stennok-Corbac* and *Stennok-Balconneill* in the same great charter. On Pont's map it is *Stinnock*. This may be derived from OE *stan-wic*, 'stony farm', but compare Stanwick (Northamptonshire), pronounced *stanik*, probably from OE *stan-wicga*, 'logan-stone', i.e., 'rocking stone'. The nearby **Stein Head**, 487370, Whithorn, may refer to the same stone. *Stein*, it is true, appears to be derived from Norse *steinn* rather than OE *stan*, 'stone, rock, boulder', but the modern pronunciation 'stane' suggests an origin in OE; the spelling may represent nothing more than an antiquarian fancy.

Shedd*ock* or **Shadd*ock***, also **Shedd*ock* Point** and **Howe Hole of Shedd*ock***, 476396, habitation, 479390, 477396, Whithorn, appears as *Schedok* in the same charter, *Schedach* in Pont. The first element may again be a personal name, although OE *scead*, *sceað*, 'boundary', is possible.

Stell*ock*, 369413, Glasserton, habitation, may be 'Stealla's fermtoun'; for the name see *ODEPN*, s.v. Stelling. Stella in Co. Durham and Northumberland however contains the dialect word *stelling*, 'cattlefold, place where cattle take shelter from the sun'.

Latin *vicus* was borrowed into OE as *wic*. Similarly the Latin plural form *castra*, 'fortress, town', was borrowed as *cæster* or *ceaster*, preserved in the names of such English places as Castor, Chester, Gloucester, or Manchester. Ekwall remarks (*ODEPN*, 88) that the meaning of this early loan-word was 'a city or walled town, originally one that had been a Roman station', but adds that 'in many cases the meaning must have been "prehistoric fort" generally. The Northumbrian names in -*chester*, for instance, cannot all denote old Roman stations --- *Caster*, -*caster* is sometimes replaced by *castle*. One example of this last development is the name Bewcastle (Cumberland), which appears during the twelfth and thirteenth centuries as *Buthecastre* and *Bothecaster*.'

A Wigtownshire example is Longcastle, preserved in **Long Castle**, 396468, Kirkinner, now only an archaeological site, **Boreland of Longcastle**, 389471, Kirkinner, habitation, **Kirkland of Longcastle**, 374474, habitation, and **Longcastle Schoolhouse**, 381478, habitation. The earliest form preserved is *Longastir* (*RMS* ii, 731, 732, 14 July 1459, 2541, 13 July 1500), *Bordland de Longestir* (*RMS* ii, 2391, 13 March 1498). The probable meaning is 'long prehistoric fort', with a possible reference to the present Long Castle or to the site marked 'Enclosure' on **Annat Hill**, 388465, 62 m., or, most probably, to a crannog in ***Dowalton Loch***, 401466, Sorbie, now drained, sometimes mentioned (*cum lacu et insulis eisdem pertinentibus*, 'with the lake and islands pertaining to the same') in documents referring to Longcastle. The 'islands' mentioned may in fact have been the remains of crannogs.

The limit of early Anglian administrative authority is perhaps indicated by Merrick, at present the name of the highest hill (2764 ft.) of a range which dominates the valley of the Cree, the river which in modern times marks the eastern boundary of Wigtownshire. The hill thus lies outside the modern boundaries. The name however is a Scandinavianized form of OE (*ge*)*mær-hrycg*, 'boundary-ridge'; compare Marrick (Yorks., N Riding). Originally it was not limited to a single hill. John MacTaggart in his *Scottish Gallovidian Encyclopedia* (London, 1824), p.340, has this entry: 'MERRICK – Five large hills or mountains in Galloway: they lay beside one another, and gradually rise, the one a little higher above the other: in the morning and evening the shadows of these hills on the level moors below seem like the fingers: hence the name Merrick, which, in the Gaelic, signifies *fingers*.' The etymology, based on the Gaelic adjective *meurach*, 'fingered' (from *meur*, *miar*, 'finger'), is fantastic, but MacTaggart at least indicates that the name was applied to a group rather than to a single hill. This seems also to be implied in Maclellan's *Description of Galloway*. He states that there are three unusually high mountains in Galloway, Cairnsmore of Fleet, Merrick and Criffel. Several hills around Merrick, however – Kirriereoch, Benyellary, Lamachan – are as high, or higher, than Cairnsmore. By Merrick Maclellan would seem to have intended the entire group. Indeed, Merrick may once have implied the entire ridge from Shalloch on Minnoch in Ayrshire to the north, as far as Cairnharrow (Anwoth) to the south, with Cairnsmore included, the whole forming an effectual hill boundary to the lands under the control of Wigtown and, in early times more particularly, Whithorn. The actual boundary may have been marked by the Skyre Burn (Anwoth parish, Kirkcudbrightshire). 'Skyre' is a variant, perhaps like Merrick a Scandinavianised form of the OE word *scir*, 'shire, district', in OE times used in something like the modern sense and also to describe a smaller district. Here it probably marks the boundary of the secular authority exercised by the Bishop of Whithorn or alternatively the ealdorman who was the royal deputy in this most westerly province of the Northumbrian kingdom.

Almost certainly the names **Whithorn**, **Wigtown, Wigg,** together with the other names in *wic*, **Longcastle**, Merrick and Skyre originated in the Anglian period, that is to say the period before about 850 AD. With others, particularly names ending in *–ton*, OE *tun*, usually best rendered 'fermtoun', no such certainty is possible; the ending remained in active use over a very long period. In the Rhinns and Luce valley it is rare, but in one instance, Tradeston, formerly a part of Stranraer, the name is self-evidently late, probably eighteenth- or early nineteenth-century. Toskarton (Stoneykirk) with its Scandinavian associations most probably belongs to the period 1050-1200. A Wigtownshire name may best be assumed to have an Anglian origin if in England parallel forms exist for which it is possible to establish a more or less certain OE provenance. Heighton, 019722, Kirkcolm, habitation, for instance, a name which I did not discuss in MacQueen 2002, is probably the same as in Heighton Street and South Heighton in Sussex, OE *Heahtun*, 'high [ferm]toun', with *heah* in the uninflected form, or '[ferm]toun by *Heah* ['the Height]' (*ODEPN*, 221, 523); compare and contrast **Loch Hempton**, 308546, Mochrum, below. Heighton may well belong to the Anglian period.

The peculiar case of **Cruggleton** (480432; Sorbie) has already been noted, as has the fact that the second element in **Wigtown** is probably not *–ton* but *-dun*. There is no early documentary evidence for **Bishopton**, 436411, Whithorn, habitation; it is obviously 'bishop's fermtoun', i.e., a fermtoun which paid its dues directly to the bishop of Whithorn and probably maintained his table. It may also have been the style of his official place of residence. On Pont's map it is *Bishoptou*(*n*), erroneously placed to the south of the burgh. The name existed in Anglo-Saxon England but there is no more than a possibility that at Whithorn it is as old as the Anglian period. Formally, it is a compound of 'bishop' and 'toun' rather than a possessive followed by its noun as in *Bishopstone*, a form not uncommon in southern England. This may suggest that the name is early.

Outon is found in **Corwar Outon** (or **Outon Corwar**), **Chapel Outon**, **Gallows Outon** and **Burgess Outon**, 440429, 448424, 451423, 452419, Whithorn, habitations, all just north of the burgh, at a slightly greater distance than **Bishopton**. The name appears as the *quatuor quarterias terre de Oton in Farinys*, 'the four land quarters of *Oton* in Farines', in a charter of Robert I, dated 20 May 1325, confirming several grants of land made by others earlier in his reign to the prior and chapter of Whithorn (*RMS* i, Appendix 1, 20). On 1 July 1451 the king (James II) confirmed the charter; here the form is *Otoun in Farnis* (*RMS* ii, 461). In July 1473 the king (James III) confirmed a charter of Roger, prior of Whithorn, in which he granted to William Douglas, canon and former prior of Whithorn, *8 merc. Terrarum mercata duarum villarum nuncupatarum Otanys, unacum crofta, antique extente*, 'the eight-merk-lands of the two vills called *Otanys*, together with a croft, of old extent' (*RMS* ii, 1134). In the post-Reformation charter already mentioned, dated 1 January 1579, the king (James VI) confirms another by which the commendator of Whithorn conveyed to James Earl of Moray (among much else) '*5 marcat. ant. ext. de Lytill Owtoun ... 5 marcat. Ant. ext. de Owtoun-Carvour*, 'the five-merk-land of old extent of *Lytill Owtoun* ... the five-merkland of old extent of *Owtoun-Carvour'*. Later in the same document *5 marcatis vocat. Outounis-chapell*, 'the five-merk-land of *Outounis-chapell'*, is mentioned as separate from the other two (*RMS* iv, 2823). The phrase 'of old extent' indicates that these lands were recorded by name in the late thirteenth century, much later than the Anglian period, but still early for Scottish place-names.

The forms indicate a derivation from OE *ut-tun*, 'out fermtoun', indicating a holding on the outskirts of Whithorn. Gaelic units of land-measurement are presupposed in the phrase *quatuor quarterias*, 'four land-quarters', indicating that the estate as a whole amounted to a davoch or ounceland, divided into four *ceathramhan*, 'quarters', which eventually became the four modern Outons (see below, c. 3(b), and MacQueen 2002, 41-5). In the last charter quoted, subdivisions of the davoch are marked by a descriptive noun or adjective or by the name of a tenant. **Chapel Outon** appears as *Outonis-chapell*. **Gallows Outon** is so called because it was the site of the burgh gallows where local malefactors were publicly executed. Chapel Outon is close to Gallows Outon, perhaps (among other things) to allow the priest to provide the last rites for condemned prisoners on their way to the gallows; see also below, chapter 4. **Burgess Outon** was the property of the burgesses of Whithorn; cf. Burgess Croft near Stranraer.

Formally, **Corwar Outon** stands a little apart. **Corwar** is Gaelic *corr bharr*, 'long hill', a name which fits the topography of the place. The combination of Gaelic and English suggests that 'Outon', the defining element, is earlier than the qualifying element 'Corwar'. If the English name is in fact the older, it may also indicate the possibility that the name Outon goes back as far as the Anglian period.

The simplex form Corwar is also found in **Corwar Hill**, 321633, Kirkcowan, 95 m., **Corwar Hill**, 387630, Penninghame, 62 m., **Corwar** and **Corwar Hill**, 451487, Sorbie, habitation; 449487, 48 m. Note how in each case English 'hill' is tautologically associated with the name. The hill remained constant while the language of the neighbourhoods changed.

Yettown Park, 475491, Sorbie, habitation, appears as 'the lands of *Yettoun*' (*RMS iv*, 764, footnote 2, 28 February 1553). Compare Yatton (Herefordshire, Somerset), OE *Geat-tun*, '[ferm]toun in a pass'. On *geat* Ekwall observes: 'The usual meaning is probably "gate" ... In Margate, Westgate, *gate* seems to refer to a natural opening in the sea wall. Sometimes OE *geat* is used of a gap in a chain of hills' (*ODEPN*, s.v. *geat*, *gæt*). Yettown Park is situated in the gap which leads down to **Innerwell Port**, 479493; Sorbie; Pont, *The Roade of Innerwall*, on Wigtown Bay.

No stream enters the sea at **Innerwell Port**; the first element is not Gaelic *inbhir*, 'confluence, mouth of a stream', as is the case, for instance, with Innermessan, 087632, Inch. Rather it is the adjective *inner*, OE *innera*, 'situated within or inside'. The second element, *-well*, is OE *wæl*, 'pool, deep place in a river or in the sea'. Symson indicates the explanation in his *Large Description of Galloway* (p.45): 'In the parish of Kirkmadroyne there is a place called Enderwell, to which ships may have recourse in time of storms'. The little bay is sheltered from the more open waters to the south by the Eggerness promontory.

Roade in Pont means 'a partly sheltered anchorage'. Symson's *Ender-* is a variant spelling of *inner*, more usually *enner*.

Broughton appears in the modern names **Broughton Mains**, 452451, Whithorn, habitation, and **Broughton Skeog**, 452440, habitation, linked by **Broughton Bridge**, 452447 over a streamlet, in its lower reaches called **Pouton Burn**. ***Old Place of Broughton***, 457451, once stood in the immediate neighbourhood. In a charter of David II dated 2 January 1366 (*RMS* i, 223) the properties appear as *terris ... de duabus Brochtounys*, 'the lands of the two Broughtons', grouped together with *terris de Scrogiltona* (a mistranscription of *Crogiltona*, 'Cruggleton'), *de Poltona* (modern **Pouton**, north of Old Place of Broughton), and *de Kythydalle* (unidentified; possibly **Kidsdale**, Glasserton parish).

Skeog in **Broughton Skeog** is probably to be connected with the Gaelic verb *sgag*, 'split, separate'. It is perhaps the past participle *sgagta*, 'split off, separated'. As noted, Broughton Skeog is separated from Broughton Mains by the Pouton Burn. For this usage, compare the English 'Several' as it appears in farm names (MacQueen 2002, 25-6).

Broughton is a common Old English place-name, with three distinct sources:

(1) OE *Broc-tun*, '[ferm]toun on a brook'
(2) OE *Burh-tun*, '[ferm]toun by a fortified manor'
(3) OE *Beorg-tun*, '[ferm]toun by a hill or barrow'

Topographically, any one of these is possible. The existence of **Broughton Bridge** suggests that the first is the most probable – one might compare Broughton in Peeblesshire – but, if ***Old Place of Broughton***, marked a site long occupied, the second also has some degree of probability. The name at any rate is Old English.

The junction of Gaelic with Old English in **Broughton Skeog** is evidence that here at least Gaelic was later in arrival than Old English.

Pouton, 465456, Sorbie, habitation, corresponds to the English Poulton, and means '[ferm]toun by a pool'. Three parallel examples are to be found in Cheshire, one in Gloucestershire, one in Kent, and three in Lancashire. The pool in question may have been in Wigtown Bay rather than the Pouton Burn. Symson (*Large Description of Galloway*, 45) describes 'a bay, call'd Polton, whereat in the months of July, August and September there uses to be a herring fishing: in some years they are so plentifull, that they are sold for five groats, or two shillings the maze (each maze contains five hundred, at sixscore to the hundred) and sometimes cheaper'.

Herring were vital for the medieval Scots economy; in the Machars one should compare **Culscadden**, 469490, Sorbie, habitation, Gaelic *cùil sgadein*, 'herring neuk' and **Lochanscadden**, 379381 Glasserton, *lochan sgadein*, 'herring lochan'; elsewhere the unexpected Garscadden, now in Glasgow. Compare too *The Nekhering* (*The Fox, the Wolf and the Cadger*), a fable by the Scottish poet Robert Henryson (c.1420-90), where the Cadger of the title is a travelling seller of herring, who carries his wares through the countryside in wickerwork creels, each probably containing a maze, suspended from a pony's back.

Myrton survives in **Myrton Castle** and **Myrton Chapel** (both now in ruins), and in **Clachan of Myrton**, and **White Loch of Myrton** (361432, 461433, 368439, habitation, 358435; Mochrum). Pont's map includes a Black Loch of Myrton, now **Blairbuy Loch**, 364415; Glasserton. The form of the name recorded in charters from the fourteenth- to the sixteenth-centuries is invariably *Mertoun* or *Mertoune* (*RMS* ii, 1134, 2128n., 2794, 2795, dated respectively 1473, 1381, 1505, 1505). In 1473 *Mertoune* paid an annual rent of 20 merks to Whithorn. In 1505 'for the easement (*asiamento*) etc. of the lieges and foreigners travelling on pilgrimage or other kinds of business to St Ninian in Candida Casa', *Mertoun* was erected into a burgh of barony for Sir Alexander McCulloch of *Mertoun*. In the same year the lands of *Mertoun* and ***Auchquhonwane*** (not identified) were incorporated into the free barony of *Mertoun* (the estate thus, presumably, becoming free of any servitude to Whithorn). **Court Hill**, 374457, Mochrum, 83 m., to the south-east of Myrton Castle, marks the site of the open-air barony court then established.

The name thus seems to be the same as the English Merton, found in cos. Durham, Norfolk, and Oxford, OE *mere-tun*, '[ferm]toun by a lake'. The lake is White Loch of Myrton.

It might seem reasonable to propose the same etymology for Merton in **Merton Hall** and **Merton Hall Moss**, 382639, habitation, 365625; Penninghame. The modern form of the name goes back to the sixteenth century. Pont's map has *Mertoun-Makke*, with the family name Mackie as second element. This element is explained in a charter dated 23 December 1506 (*RMS* ii, 3018), in which the lands of *Myretown-Makke* are taken from John Makke of *Myretoun* and restored as a free barony to Andrew Herries, Lord Terregles. The official name of the barony then briefly became *Myretoun-Heris*. Included within the barony, incidentally, were two places already mentioned, **Ochiltree** (*Uchiltre*) and **Culbratten** (*Culbertone*). A few months later, on 16 September 1507, John Makke and his wife Margaret Auchinleck recovered the lands of *Mertoun*, but not the barony, when Herries was outlawed and driven from Scotland (*RMS* ii, 3134) – whence, no doubt, Pont's form of the name. In an earlier charter dated 10 December 1477 (*RMS* ii, 1337), *Myretoun* was erected into a burgh of barony for John Kennedy of Blairquhan (near Maybole in Carrick). At the same time (*RMS* ii, 1336) the lands of *Frethride*, *Skeche* (**Skaith**, 374664, Penninghame, habitation), and *Myretone* were incorporated into the free barony of Myretoun 'for the voluntary labours and services done for the King by the said John in the capture and return of certain rebels put to the horn by the king'. The reference is probably to some event in the campaign undertaken in 1476 'to execute the forfeiture pronounced by parliament on John of the Isles, formerly Earl of Ross and Lord of the Isles, "traitor and rebel"' (Macdougall 1982, 122). John Kennedy was afterwards (in 1484) a conservator of the truce between James III of Scotland and Richard III of England (ibid, 214).

Kennedy had himself come into possession when on 21 March 1474 Sir Robert Colville of Barnweil (near Symington, Ayrshire) conceded to him the lands of *Myretoun* and *Frethrid* (*RMS* ii, 1162).

On 1 June 1486 the king granted Andrew Herries the lands of Terregles and much else, including the lands of Barnweil, Symington and *Myretoun*, previously held by Colville (*RMS* ii, no.1654). There is no mention of Kennedy.

The ownership of the lands thus has a complicated and somewhat obscure history, but on one point at least it is straightforward. The form *Mertoun* is found only in documents later than 1506. Earlier ones have *Myretoun*, or a close variant. The first element, it would seem, is not OE *mere*, 'lake' (in any case, there is no substantial body of water in the neighbourhood), but Old Norse *myrr*, 'wet swampy ground, a boggy place', or its Middle English and Early Scots derivative *myre*, modern English *mire*, with the same meaning. Merton is thus 'fermtoun by a mire or [peat]bog (i.e., Merton Hall Moss)'. The name is probably no earlier than the eleventh or twelfth century. The modern spellings Merton (Penninghame) and Myrton (Mochrum) more or less invert the original meaning.

***Frethride*,** already mentioned but apparently no longer extant, is 'free third', with the metathesis of the second *-r-* characteristic of Middle Scots; compare *Middilthrid*, 'middle third', five examples of which are to be found in *RMS* ii, one (1206, 2590) in the Stewartry, one (1890) in Stirlingshire, and three (2584, 2662, 3347, 3748) in Perthshire. *Nethirthrid* also occurs in the Stewartry (1208), close to Middilthrid, both forming parts of the lands of Kirkcormack (Kelton). Milnthird (Kelton), 'mill third', probably completes the trinity. 'Third' is probably a rendering into English of Gaelic *trian* with the same meaning; compare Trinafour, Perthshire, *trian a phùir*, 'pasture-third'. One-third of a davoch or ounceland is indicated. With its Scots form and Gaelic background the name Frethride is probably no older than the twelfth century.

Skaith, 374664, Penninghame, habitation, may represent a Scandinavianized form of OE *sceat*, 'strip of land', later 'piece of land left untilled and overgrown with trees or plants' (*ODEPN*, s.v.). Early forms are *Skeich* (*RMS* ii, 1025, 4 June 1471); *Skeche* (*ibid*., 1336, 10 December 1477); *Skeath* (*ibid*., 2410, 27 May 1498); *Skeoth* (*ibid*., 2636, 29 March 1502); *Skeich* (*ibid*., 2943, 27 February 1506); *Skeath* (*ibid*., 3040, 29 January 1507). In several of these forms *–th* has been confused with *–ch*, as often happens in medieval manuscripts. Compare too **Skate Hill**, 432525, Kirkinner, 23 m., mentioned below; also **Skate**, 357485, Mochrum, habitation, together with the associated **Skate Cottage**, 355480, habitation; **Skate Moor**, 3648.

Ravenstone is found in **Ravenstone Castle**, **Ravenstone Mains** and **Ravenstone Moss**, 409441, habitation, 415441, habitation, 406426; Whithorn. In Pont the form is *Remistown*, *Remistoun*; the latter form also being found much earlier (*RMS* ii, 12, 25 October 1424; *RMS* iii, 2266, 5 February 1541). Maxwell noted that the local pronunciation was 'Reimston' and continued 'This name has nothing to do with Raven or Rafn; the modern form is purely fanciful and misleading, the original being preserved in the local pronunciation'. He is probably wrong. The OE word for 'raven' had two forms, *hræfn* and *hremm*, the second resulting from a double process of assimilation, *hræfn* becoming *hræmn*, which in turn became *hremm*. Two passages of Anglo-Saxon poetry illustrate the process. Line 61 of *The Battle of Brunnanburh* has *hræfn*:

Leton him behindan hraw bryttigean
salowigpadan þone sweartan **hræfn**
hyrnednebban –

'They left behind them to enjoy the carrion the swart raven, dark-plumed and horn-beaked'

The poem was probably written in the year 937. A later poem, *The Battle of Maldon*, was written in 991. Line 106 preserves *hremm* in plural form:

Þær wearð hream ahafen, **hremmas** *wundon,*
earn æses georn –

'Then clamour arose, ravens wheeled, the eagle greedy for carrion'

The *rem-* of *Remistoun* is thus probably a development of OE *hremm*, while *raven-* in *Ravenstone* comes from *hræfn*. The earliest instance of *Ravenstone* known to me is on the 1782 Ainslie map, but some sense that *rem-* and *raven-* were equivalent must have survived from Old English times. The name Ravenscleugh (Roxburgh) may provide a parallel. In a charter dated 7 June 1568 (*RMS* iv, 1819) it is *Ravynniscleuch*, but in another dated 14 December 1587 (*ibid.*, 2752) it is *Ramsecleuchis*. Compare too Ramsbury in Wiltshire, in a charter dated 905 called *æcclesia Corvinensis*, 'raven church'.

It is likely that the name refers, not to a bird, but to someone called *Hræfn* or *Hremm*, '*Hremm*'s fermtoun'. The second element is *-toun*, not

-*stone*, which would have appeared as -*stane*. As in modern English, -*s*- indicates the possessive.

Loch Hempton, 308546, Mochrum, is shown on Pont's map as *L*[*och*] *Dyrhempen*, where *–hempen* may be a corrupt form of *-hempton.* No farm or settlement called Hempton now exists, but it is possible that the loch was originally named for such a place. Pont's form would then mean 'Loch of Hempton wood'. *Dyr-* is Gaelic *doire*, 'oak-grove, thicket'. The name Hempton is found in Gloucestershire and Oxfordshire, and is probable derived from OE *Hean-tune*, the dative or locative case of *Hea-tun*, 'high [ferm]toun'. Loch Hempton stands well above sea-level, but amidst an extensive flat peat-bog, so this derivation does not seem appropriate. The first element of another Hempton, this time in Norfolk, is the Anglo-Saxon proper name *Hemma*. This might be the derivation, but there is no way of proving it. Maxwell thought that the name might represent OE *hamtun,* as in Northampton and Southampton, and that it might refer to the nearby Mochrum Castle (**Old Place of Mochrum**, 307541, Mochrum, habitation) – more probably, one must add, to an earlier building or settlement on the same site. Old Place of Mochrum, however, is much closer to Mochrum Loch than to Loch Hempton. The etymology remains uncertain.

Milton is found in **High** and **Low Milton**, **Milton Fell**, **Milton Bridge**, **Mull Hill of Milton** and **Milton Point** (318475, 318467, both habitations, 314477, 127 m., 319461, 312463, 52 m., 315462; Mochrum). In the immediate neighbourhood are **Old Mill Burn** and **Old Mill House**, 322472, habitation. Sixteenth-century charters mention *dimediatem suam molendini de Arewllane, Myltoun de Arewllan nuncupat.*, 'his half of the mill of Airyolland, called *Myltoun* of Airyolland' (*RMS* iv, 265, 24 December 1548); *duodecimam partem ... 5 libratarum de Litill Arreullane vocat. Mylntoun, dimedietatis molendini de Mochrome ibi situati*, 'the twelfth part ... of Little Airyolland called *Mylntoun* and [his] half of Mochrum mill situated there' (*ibid.*, 2208, 19 March 1574); *Mylnetoun* (*ibid.*, 2285, 20 July 1574). Airyolland is the name of a neighbouring farm (see MacQueen 2002, 39-40); it would seem that Milton was also known as Little Airyolland, and was the site of the mill for Mochrum parish or barony. The forms represent OE *mylen-tun*, 'mill [ferme]toun'. The millwheel was turned by the water of the Old Mill Burn.

There is another Milton in the Rhinns parish of Kirkcolm (MacQueen 2002, 6, 79). Others, now lost, were in the barony of ***Frethird*** (*RMS* ii, 2943, 27 February 1506) and in Kirkinner parish (*RMS* iv, 2866, 22 May 1579). In this last the five-merkland of *Mylntoun* is associated with the five-merkland of *Skayth*, names commemorated today in **Milton Hill** and **Skate Hill**, just south of **East** and **West Mains of Baldoon** (428522, 432525, 431527, habitation, 429527, habitation, Kirkinner). The mill was probably on the site of the modern **Mildriggan Mill**, 441521, Kirkinner, on the **Maltkiln Burn**. The element *–driggan* in Mildriggan is probably derived from the Gaelic verb *driog*, 'distil' – 'distillation mill'. The distillation of whisky from malt, supplied by the mill and dried in the maltkiln, is the dominant factor in this group of names.

Orchardton is found in **Orchardton Farm**, **Orchardton Hill**, **Orchardton Bungalow** and **Orchardton Cottages**, 458498, habitation, 457497, 47 m., 455495, habitation, 452491, habitation, Sorbie. In Pont the form is *Orchardtoun*, which may be the same as the *croftam vocatam* the Orcheart *per dominum de Jardinis occupat*[*am*], 'the croft called the Orcheart occupied by Master Jardine' (*RMS* iv, 2823, 1 January 1579). There is another Orchardton in the Stewartry (Rerwick parish), one in Kincardine and one in Aberdeenshire. The name may originally have been a compound of OE *ortgeard*, 'an enclosed piece of ground for the purposes of horticulture', and *tun*. 'Orchard' uncompounded appears as an English place-name in Devon and Somerset; the compound 'Orchardleigh' is in Somerset; documentary evidence shows that this, and one of the two Somerset 'Orchards', goes back to Anglo-Saxon times. A miracle story involving an orchard in this sense is narrated in the eighth-century *Miracula Nynie Episcopi*, chapter 7. The word 'orchard', however, later invariably indicating a place where fruit-trees rather than herbs and vegetables are grown, long remained active in place-name formation. There is thus no more than a possibility that the name is as old as the Anglian period.

Glasserton, 421387, Glasserton, habitation, the name of a hamlet as well as a parish, is puzzling. Pont has *Glastoun*, a form probably indicating a pronunciation like Maxwell's '*pron*. Glaiston'. Symson (*Large*

Description of Galloway, 50) has 'Glasserton, commonly called Glaston'. Earlier forms, *Glassartoune*, *Glassertoune* (*RMS* ii, 663, 13 January 1459; 1134, dated 1473), come closer to the modern spelling. Possibly two forms of the name existed, one with, and one without, internal *-er-*. If the first element is OE *glæs*, 'glass', the *-er-* form would indicate 'a worker in glass, a glazier'. The meaning would then be 'fermtoun where a worker in glass lives'. Compare in England Glascote (Staffs.), 'hut where glass is made'; also in a slightly different sense Glasbury (Herts.), perhaps '*burg* with glass windows'. In Anglo-Saxon times drinking vessels were sometimes made of glass and glass windows were to be found in major churches, like that at Whithorn; see Hill 1997, 167, 327; for glass vessels, *ibid.* 297-8, 310-13.

On Pont's map **Carleton**, 391378, Glasserton, habitation, is *Karltoun*. Maxwell quotes a form *Karlaton* from a charter dated 1250 which he does not identify. This fairly obviously is the same as the many English *Carl*(*e*)*ton*s, from ON *Karlatun*, 'which', as Ekwall remarks (*ODEPN*, s.v.), 'usually no doubt means "the **Tun** of the free men or peasants". The name *Karlatun* is never found in Scandinavia, and very likely *Carl(e)ton* is in most cases due to Scandinavianization of OE *Ceorlatun*; cf. Charlton, Chorlton'. Gillian Fellows-Jensen accepts that this applies to the Wigtownshire Carleton, noting also that in Kirkcolm parish there is a second Wigtownshire example, which I have not been able to identify, together with another in the Stewartry, Borgue parish ('Scandinavians in Dumfriesshire and Galloway: the Place-Name Evidence', Oram and Stell 1991, 86). Carleton is also found in Carleton Castle, together with Carleton Mains and Little Carlton (133895, 138137, 133895, all habitations) in adjoining Carrick.

Under *Charlton* (*ODEPN*, 91) Ekwall further remarks: 'OE *ceorl* ['churl'] means "a freeman of the lowest rank, a free peasant". But it is quite possible that already in OE times the word had come to be used also of a villein. Whether the name *Ceorlatun* means "**Tun** of the free peasants" or "**Tun** of the villeins", it suggests that manorialism had made a good deal of advance in OE times, for even "**Tun** of the free peasants" presupposes that there were villages not held by freemen'. In terms of Anglo-Saxon history, the Anglian period in the Machars is relatively early; it is therefore likely that the *ceorlas* of Carleton were free peasants. This leaves open the possibility, even the likelihood, that other names in *–ton*, belonging to the same period, mark places where the people were not free, regarded simply as part of the lands on which they lived. It is perhaps significant that the majority of these names refer, not to persons, but to features, natural or artificial, in the landscape.

None of the names so far discussed belong to the oldest stratum of English names, called by Ekwall and others 'folk-names' – names, that is to say, originally attached to the inhabitants of a particular place, or alternatively to a kin-group, a clan, with an assumed common ancestor or leader. The folk-name afterwards became the name of the place where the 'folk' had lived. In the modern form of the names this is signified by the suffix *–ing* or *–ings*, shortened from OE *–ingas*, meaning in effect 'people' or 'clan'. Thus Blything (Suffolk) means 'people (clan) living on the river Blyth', Blickling (Norfolk) 'Blicla's people (clan)', Hastings (Sussex) 'Hæsta's people (clan)'. We do not know who Blicla or Hæsta were, but these names belong to the time of the earliest Anglo-Saxon settlements, say 450-600 AD. There is no certain example in Scotland where probably there was no Anglo-Saxon presence at so early a date.

Names ending in *–ham*, 'home, homestead', are sometimes as early as those in *–ingas*, but the word remained in active use for place-names over a much longer period. Sometimes it is combined with an element *–ing-* or *–inga-*, perhaps the same as that found in *-ingas*, perhaps simply an OE connective particle implying 'associated with' or 'called after'. English examples are Birmingham, probably 'homestead of the family or followers of a man called Beorma', and Whittingham (Lancashire and Northumberland) or Whicham (Cumberland), both meaning 'homestead of the family or followers of a man called Hwita'. Again, neither personal name is known to history. There is a Scottish Whittinghame (East Lothian), which may be connected with the Northumbrian Whittingham, also Coldingham (Berwickshire), 'homestead of the family or followers of a man called Colud', and Tyninghame (East Lothian), 'homestead of the people on the river Tyne'.

Two poorly-documented Wigtownshire names may follow this pattern. One is the parish-name **Penninghame**, in 1532 *Pennynghame*

(*RMS* iii, 1138). The name also survives in **Penninghame Clachan** and **Kirk** and **Mains of Penninghame**, 411612, 405607, Penninghame, habitations. On Pont's map the **Bishop Burn** is called *Pennygha*[*m*] *Burn*, presumably because it marked the parish boundary. **Penninghame House** and **Penninghame Home Farm**, 383698, 380693, Penninghame, habitations, lie some seven miles to the north. The etymology is uncertain, but, despite some scholarly doubts, there remains a possibility that the final element is Anglian *–ingaham*.

The same possibility exists for **Cunninghame**, 384558, Wigtown, habitation, on the left bank of the Bladnoch some three miles above the burgh. I have not found any early forms.

OE *treow*, 'tree' is common as the final element in English place-names. Examples are Coventry, 'Cofa's tree', and Daventry, 'Dafa's tree'. **Prestrie**, 465378, Whithorn, habitation, is a Wigtownshire example, in Pont *Prestry*, earlier *Preistrie* (*RMS* iv, 2823, 1 January 1579), OE *preost*, 'priest, parson', compounded with *treow*, 'priests' tree'. Ekwall remarks: 'Names of this kind refer to some prominent tree, sometimes one with religious associations ... sometimes one remarkable for its size ... The first element is frequently a personal name. In these cases the tree was probably often one marking a meeting-place, and the first element may well be the name of a lawman' (*ODEPN*, 458). The tree at Prestrie may have been one where priests assembled for some religious purpose, or may have been the site of an open-air religious court.

Mochrum is a parish name, found also in **Old Place of Mochrum**, 307541, Mochrum, habitation, on **Mochrum Loch**, 302530, Mochrum, and in **Kirk of Mochrum**, 347463, Mochrum, habitation, a hamlet some 6 1/2 miles to the south. **Mochrum Park**, 370571, Wigtown, habitation, was built by Sir William Dunbar, 7th baronet of Mochrum (1812-89), and named to commemorate the lost estates of his family. There is another Mochrum in the Stewartry (Parton parish). Early Wigtownshire forms are *Mochrom* (*RMS* i, Appendix 1, 20, 20 May 1326), *Mochrum*, *Muchrum* (*ibid.*, Appendix 2, 623, 1329), *Mouchroume* (*RMS* ii, 461, 1 July 1451), *Mochrome*, *Mochrum* (*ibid.*, 2464, 31 October 1498). The second element may be OE *rum*, 'room', probably also 'clearing', found in Dendron (Lancs.), 'clearing in a valley'. The word however also exists in Old

Old Place of Mochrum ('damp muddy clearing'), c.1870

Old Place of Mochrum today

Norse and Old Swedish. The first element seems to be the adjective *moch*, 'damp, moist, muggy', extant only in Middle and later Scots, but perhaps cognate with English dialectal *moky*, 'foggy, murky' and with words in the Scandinavian languages. 'Scandinavian cognates are apparently Swedish dialectal *moket*, "cloudy, hazy", Old Swedish *muk*, "damp", Danish *mug*, "mildew", Norwegian *muggen*, "fusty, mouldy" ... the root meaning being "wet and decaying" (*SND*, *s.v. moch*). **Mochrum** would thus be 'damp, muggy clearing', particularly appropriate to the site of **Old Place of Mochrum**, situated in the middle of a peat-bog, with **Mochrum Loch** and four other smaller lochs in the immediate neighbourhood. The name may have an origin in OE, but one in Old Norse seems likelier.

With only a few exceptions, the possible OE names so far discussed have been habitation names. **Burrow Head**, 457340, Whithorn, in Pont *Burrow Head*, is descriptive of a feature, part natural, part artificial. Both elements are OE; *Burrow* is *burh*, 'fort, fortified settlement', *Head* is *heafod*, 'head', extended to mean variously 'headland, summit, upper end, source of a stream' – here clearly 'headland'. OE *burh* 'is a very common element in [OE] place-names. The meaning is usually "fortified place, fort". Very often the reference is to a Roman or other pre-English fort' (*ODEPN*, *sv. burg*, *burh*). Here the reference is to the three Iron Age forts on the headland itself. The name means 'headland of the forts'.

On the whole, OE names belong to the Machars rather than the Moors. If the chief apparent exceptions, **Penninghame** and **Cunninghame**, in fact show the suffix *–ingaham*, recognised as a relatively early feature, Anglian settlement may have begun at the head of Wigtown Bay, only afterwards extending southward to form a cluster round Whithorn. But, fairly clearly, Whithorn soon became the focus of settlement, a settlement that was relatively dense. For some centuries Old English must have been the dominant speech, at least of the Machars, in marked contrast with the situation in the Moors and the Rhinns.

Chapter 3

The Chronology of some Early Gaelic Names

In early times most people lived by subsistence farming in small scattered settlements, which gave rise to some of the most interesting local place-names. The Scots word for such settlements was 'fermtoun'; in Welsh it was *tref*, in Old English *tun*, both of which have already been discussed. Gaelic made use of several words, each with a slightly differing connotation. I shall discuss them individually.

(a) *achadh*

The word *achadh* is usually translated 'field'. This, however, is somewhat misleading. A modern farm includes several, or many, individual fields used for various purposes, but each part of the central farm, run by a single farmer or farm-manager. Before the eighteenth-century Agricultural Revolution things were very different. The fermtoun, rather than farm, was a collective enterprise, worked, often by an extended family group, who lived on the single 'field' which they cultivated, in later times at least, by 'the system of run-rig, whereby, each year, each tenant was allocated several detached portions and *rigs* in the 'field' by lot and rotation, so that each would share in turn in the more fertile areas' (*SND*). The major division was between the 'infield', where crops were grown and where people lived, and 'outfield', uncultivated ground where the animals of the fermtoun grazed and were milked, especially during the months of growth and harvest. The term *achadh* implies such a settlement or its even more archaic predecessor.

The term figures in place-names from the earliest recorded times. Under the Year of the World 4334 (AD 130), for instance, the *Annals of Ulster* record the battle of *Achad Lethderg*, 'field of the red half' or 'side'. This may not be the name of a settlement, but that given to the actual battle-field. More certain is the reference under 487 to the death of St Mel, a bishop, in *Ardachadh* (*Arddachuth*), 'high field', the modern Ardagh (N2169; Co. Longford), a place-name also found elsewhere in Ireland with a double Wigtownshire parallel (below, p.). Under 521 we find the birth of Cainnech of *Achad Bó*, modern Aghavoe (S3384; Co. Laoighis), 'field of the cow'. Cainnech was a friend of St Columba, and in Adomnan's *Life of Columba*, written before 700, there is a reference (63a) to Cainnech 'being in his own monastery, which is in Latin called "field of the cow", and in Irish *Ached bou*' (Anderson, *Columba*, 113). Perhaps significantly, the field is that of a single cow, not a herd; the monastery was deliberately built on an impoverished property. Hundreds of other early names in *achadh* are listed in Hogan's *Onomasticon* (Hogan 1910) and in the first fascicule of the more recent *Historical Dictionary of Gaelic Placenames* (*HDGP*).

As used in place-names, *achadh* is pretty well equivalent to Welsh *tref*. Conceivably it sometimes replaced the earlier term.

Nicolaisen (Nicolaisen 1976, 125) demonstrates that *achadh* continued for a very long time to be used in the formation of Scottish place-names. In the Moors and Machars most examples seem likely to be early, but one or two are certainly late.

As noted in MacQueen 2002, 74-5, surviving names in *achadh* probably for the most part represent older servile communities, worked by *nativi* or 'neyfs', thirled to the land and its lord by birth and blood.

Ardachie, 322631, Kirkcowan, habitation, *Ardauch* (*RMS* iii, 1030; 22 May 1531) is *ard achadh*, 'high field', the same as Ardagh, where St Mel was bishop. **Ardachie Fell**, 322644; Kirkcowan, 135 m., is about a mile to the north and may mark the limit of the Ardachie outfield.

Maxwell lists another **Ardachie**, which I have not been able to locate, in Whithorn parish.

Garwachie Moor, 345696, Penninghame, and **Garwachie Lochs**, 346689, take their names from a lost fermtoun, *RMS* ii, 3018; 23 December 1506, *Garvake*; 3134, 16 September 1507, *Garwachy*, Pont *Garuacchy*: *garbh achadh*, 'rough field'.

In **Killauchie Hill**, 341621, Penninghame, 72 m., the first element is probably *cùil*, 'corner': *cùil achaidh*, 'corner of the field'.

These names follow the older Celtic practice by which the qualifying adjective preceded the noun.

In **Auchengallie**, 339485, Mochrum, habitation, the defining final element is probably the surname Gallie or Gailey, from *gallda*, 'foreign, strange, unable to speak Gaelic'. If this is so, the place-name is almost certainly late. *Auchen-* usually represents *achadh*, followed by the genitive of the definite article, represented by *–en*, prefixed to the qualifying noun. In late names, however, it is sometimes followed by personal names in the genitive and even before adjectives. Nicolaisen (Nicolaisen 1976, 125) remarks: 'Whether this development took place during the end-phase of Gaelic in these parts, when inflexional features were breaking down, or whether it should be ascribed to the process of anglicisation is difficult to say, but the most plausible general explanation would be that a bilingual situation was responsible for such changes'. The meaning is 'Gallie's field'. It may well be significant that any Gallie was, almost by definition, ignorant of Gaelic usage.

Maxwell suggests that **Auchleand**, 415588, Wigtown, habitation, Pont, *Achleaun*, is *achadh leathann*, 'broad field'. The extent of the fermtoun is shown by a number of dependent names, **Wood of Auchleand**, 405597, Pont, *Wood of Auchleun*, **Auchleand Moor**, 405583, **Auchleand Croft**, 411591, **Auchleand Cottage**, 418585, perhaps also **Drum*lane* Hill**, 407585. It is possible that the second element is not *leathann*, but an abbreviated form of the surname MacLean, mac Ghill' Eathain, 'son of the servant of (St) John'. Pont's spellings would support such an etymology. If this is so, the MacLean in question was thirled to a church dedicated to St John.

These are the only names in *achadh* which I have been able to identify. Maxwell records four others which seem to have disappeared since his time:

Auchie, Kirkcowan, is the simplex *achadh*, 'field'.

Auchess, Kirkcowan, looks as if it might be *achadh an easa*, 'field of the cataract, waterfall'.

The final element in ***Auchengilshie***, Kirkinner, Pont *Achingilshy*, is obscure. I find Maxwell's *achadh na gìolche*, 'broom field', unconvincing.

Auchnabrack, Mochrum, is probably *achadh breac*, 'speckled field'; cf. Auchabreck, 100417, Kirkmaiden. It is an example of the late solecism *Auchen-* + adjective; cf. Auchenbrack, 767964, Tynron, Dumfriesshire, habitation. Johnson-Ferguson (Johnson-Ferguson 1935, 123) treats the first element of this last as the plural *achaidhean*, 'fields', but this is unlikely, particularly in view of the highly-specialized meaning of *achadh* in place-names.

Only nine place-names from the Moors and Machars contain *achadh* as an element. In the smaller area of the Rhinns and Luce valley there are twenty-two (MacQueen 2002, 74-7), only one of which, Auchinfad, Old Luce), possibly *achadh fada*, 'long field', seems from its form to be late (but see MacQueen 2002, 70). This probably reflects some difference between the two areas in social circumstances, possibly also in date of settlement.

To be distinguished from the names previously discussed is **Auchness**, stressed on the first syllable and surviving as **Auchness**, 399434; Glasserton, habitation, the related **Auchness Moss**, (394441, and the more distant, perhaps unrelated, **Auchness Hill**, 391412; **Auchness Hill**, 335584, Kirkcowan, 52 m., and **Auchness Wood**, 341583; **Auchness Hill**, 357584, Wigtown, 42 m.. Auchness is *each-innis*, 'horse-meadow'. Maxwell remarks 'Many pieces of land in Galloway are named Auchness, although not so marked in the Ordnance Survey maps'. The name is to be associated with the celebrated breed of Galloway naigs.

(b) *dabhach*, *peighinn*, *ceathramh*.

In charters land-valuations are usually expressed in terms of the merk, in predecimal coinage 13/4, two-thirds of the pound Scots. The merk was the basis for a land-valuation usually described as the Auld Extent, the origins of which go back to inquisitions carried out in feudal times, much later than the period now under discussion.

In the earlier years of Gaelic settlement land values for holdings by freemen, who paid rent, were assessed in terms of the subdivision of the ounce of silver into twenty silver pennies. Such assessments are sometimes commemorated by such place-name elements as *peighinn*, 'penny-land', assessed at a penny, *leith-pheighin*, assessed at a halfpenny, or *feòirlinn*, *fàirdean*, 'farthing-land', assessed at one-fourth of a penny. *Ceathramh*, 'quarter-land', was assessed at one-quarter of an ounce of silver, five pennies. The lands so described were all, it should be noted, fermtouns; the terms, that is to say, have much the same reference as *achadh*, but also indicate the rate at which the holding was assessed. There is a greater likelihood that the tenants were freemen.

The name for the ounceland was *dabhach*, usually transcribed 'davach', literally 'a large tub or vat', in place-names usually represented by *–doch* or *–doach*. In the Moors and Machars there is only one doubtful example, **Balcullendoch**, 322764, Penninghame, not now a habitation, perhaps 'fermtoun of the holly-davoch'. If this is so, the second element, -*cullen*-, is Gaelic *cuilionn*, 'holly', a word which often occurs in Scottish place-names. The element *Bal*- will be discussed later.

It is also possible that -*cull*- is Gaelic *cùil*, 'corner' or *cùl*, back', with -*en*- the definite article; 'fermtoun in the corner', or 'at the back of the davoch'; see below, chapter 5.

Of *peighinn* not many traces remain. In **Penkiln**, 479477, Sorbie, habitation, the first element is *peighinn*, the second *cillín*, diminutive of *cill*, 'monastic cell, church'; *peighinn na cillín*, 'penny-land of the little church'; i.e., what in more recent times would have been termed the glebe. Joyce (Joyce 1913, 411) remarks: '*Killeen*. There are upwards of eighty places with this name all over Ireland, and about eighty others of which it forms the first part. In by far the greater number of these cases the name is *Cillin* [Killeen], 'little church'; but in a few it is *Coillin* [Culleen], 'little wood' or 'underwood', equivalent to Culleen elsewhere.' For Penkiln either etymology is possible, but its proximity to **Kirkmadrine**, 475483, Sorbie, makes *cillín* the more probable. The diminutive is applied to the church perhaps by comparison to the much larger church of Whithorn, some five-and-a-half miles to the south.

Penkiln Burn, 411665, Minigaff, Kirkcudbrightshire, a tributary of the Cree, may have the same etymology. As Maxwell notes, 'It flows under the walls of Minigaff parish church'. The form in Pont however is *Poolkill*, 'church burn', with a different first element and no diminutive form.

Rispain, 432398, Whithorn, habitation, Pont *Rispin*, is a compound of *riasg*, 'marsh, bogland, moor', and *peighinn*; 'bog penny-land'. Pont places it immediately south of *Loch of Apleby* (Appleby). The loch is now drained, but at one time the surrounding land would certainly have been bog.

There are no other reasonably certain examples. The names **Pen Hill** and **Penny Hill**, (409475, 68 m., 374527, 67 m., Kirkinner, may

Penkiln ('penny-land of the little church' - i.e. Kirkmadrine)

be based on *peighinn*. Pont includes on his map ***Fourtypenyland***, near **Barnbarroch**, 398515, Kirkinner, habitation, but this belongs to a later dispensation. In pre-decimal coinage, forty pennies were three shillings and fourpence, one quarter of a merk.

There are now no examples of names in *leith-pheighinn* or *feòirlinn/fàirdean* in the Moors and Machars. Pont places ***Ferdingrewy*** in the extreme north of his Wigtownshire map; the first element here is *fàirdean*, the second may be the Galloway surname MacGarva, 'son of Gairbheith', with initial *Mac*-dropped and metathesis of *-r-*.

Surviving examples of *ceathramh* are more frequent, but it is clear that over the centuries, and even in quite recent times, their number has decreased. In the following list I include several names quoted by Maxwell, whose book appeared in 1930, but which are unrecorded on the modern map. Even so, the list is not a long one.

The simplex form *ceathramh* does not appear in place-names. Usually it is the first, unstressed, element in a compound. Sometimes in early documents it appears as *Kerrow*- or *Keri/y*-, but more usually it has been reduced to *Kir*- or *Ker*-. If it is the second element, with initial *c*- aspirated to *ch*-, it usually appears as -[*e*]*rie* or -[*e*]*ry*. There is some possibility of confusion with *àirigh* as unstressed second element in a compound name.

Meikle Killantrae, 351454, Mochrum, habitation, appears in a charter dated 16 May 1557 as *Mekill Kerintra* (*RMS*, iv, 1173), i.e., *ceathramh na traighe*, 'quarter-land of, beside, the seashore', with Scots *meickle*, 'big', prefixed. The modern farm is some distance from the shore; the name better fits **High** and **Low Killantrae**, 328461, 332457, Mochrum, both habitation, both of which are situated on the edge of Luce Bay; compare and contrast **Landberrick**, 363455, discussed in chapter 2, and **North Landberrick**, 367456, habitation, both of which lie further inland than **Meikle Killantrae**.

Kirbreen survives today only in **Kirbreen Hill**, 378533, Kirkinner, 69 m., Pont *Keribroyn*. Perhaps 'Brown's quarter-land'.

Garchew (stressed on first syllable), 340758, Penninghame, habitation; Pont, *Garchery*; **Garchew Wood**, 338753: *garbh cheathramh*, 'rough quarter-land'.

Kirkcalla, 305747, Penninghame, habitation, lies to the west of **Loch Ochiltree**, 315745, Penninghame. On older O.S. maps a church-site is marked, which has disappeared from later editions. In Pont the name is *Kraigaulay*. The second element seems to be the Galloway surname variously written McCalla, McCallay, McCalley, McCallie, a form of Macauley, but with the prefixed Mac or Mc dropped. If this is so, the first element is more likely to be *ceathramh* than *kirk*. '[Mc]Calla's quarter-land'. The form in Pont suggests that it may actually be *creag*, 'rock' and that the meaning is '[Mc]Calla's crag', although this seems unlikely.

I have not identified ***Kircloy*** (Mochrum), listed by Maxwell. The second element is probably a shortened version of the surname McCloy; '[Mc]Cloy's quarter-land'.

I can find no trace of ***Kirkhobble***, placed by Maxwell in Penninghame parish and by him identified as ***Kerychappell***, on Pont's map situated north-east of *Vchiltry* [Ochiltree] and south of *Glenbarranach*, a name now represented by **Glenvernoch Fell**, 338743, 184 m. The name seems to be *ceathramh a' chapuill*, 'horse quarter-land'.

Maxwell places a ***Kirminnoch*** in Kirkinner parish, but I have not been able to locate it. He identifies it with *Kerowmanach*, *ceathramh nam manach*, 'quarter-land of the monks', recorded in a charter of 27 February1506 (*RMS*, ii, 2943) and as *Kerimanach* in Pont. These forms however refer to Kirminnoch, 123580, Inch, habitation; see MacQueen 2002, 43. The Kirkinner example more probably is *ceathramh meadhonach*, 'middle quarter-land).

Kirvennie, 415556, Wigtown, habitation, Pont *Korymny*, is obscure. The first element is probably *ceathramh*. Pont's form is corrupt.

Kirwar (Mochrum), represented on the OS map by **Kirwar Plantation**, 288509, is *ceathramh a' bharr*, 'quarter-land of the top, height'. The reference may be to the nearby **Mochrum Fell**, 197 m.

Kirwaugh, 405541, Kirkinner, habitation, appears to be the same as the *Kerywachor* on Pont's Wigtownshire map. Maxwell attributes to Pont the form *Kirriwauchop*. *Kerywachor* might be a corrupt form of *Kerywachop*. Other early forms quoted by Maxwell are *Kerwalcok*, *Carwalcok*, *Kerowaltok*. All these forms may presuppose as second element the Dumfriesshire surname Waugh or Wauchope. Black (Black

1946, 805) quotes from *The House of Glendinning*: 'The common border name of Waugh is an abbreviation of Wauchope, the Waughs are sprung from the Wauchopes and have the same arms'. The meaning is thus 'quarter-land belonging to someone named Waugh or Wauchope'.

Gargrie, 283524, Mochrum, habitation, Pont *Gargry*, on **Gargrie Moor**, near **Throne of Gargrie**, 285528, 107 m., is *garg-cheathramh*, 'rough quarter-land'. In Old Irish the adjective *garg* had much the same meaning as the more familiar *garb*, *garbh*. In the same area as Gargrie, Pont marks ***Garcherow***, *garbh-cheathramh*, also 'rough quarter-land', perhaps represented by the modern **Garheugh**, 272503, habitation, and **Garheugh Fell**, 277515, 102 m.

Craighalloch, which appears in **Fell of Craighalloch**, 319547, Mochrum, 98 m., and **Craighalloch Moor**, 3354, is in Pont *Keryhalloch*, habitation: *ceathramh an teallaich*, 'quarter-land of the blacksmith's forge'. As noted in the discussion of Challoch, below, chap. 6, forges were usually situated near the summit of a hill.

Cairndoon, 380389, Glasserton, habitation; *RMS* ii, 1134, July 1473, *Gerivindone* (for *Cerivindone*); **Cairndoon Bank**, 391391, habitation; **Low Cairndoon**, 391390, habitation: *ceathramh in dùin*, 'quarter-land of the fort'. The reference may be to the archaeological site marked *homestead*, 379387, on the OS map.

Pont also has ***Kerychappell***, already mentioned, above Wood of Cree, and ***Kerenwanach*** on the coast south of Wigtown, all apparently formed from *ceathramh*.

Kerenwanach is *ceathramh an mhanaich*, 'quarter-land of the monk, friar', with *an*, the older form of the Scottish-Gaelic genitive-singular masculine article, preserved. The Wigtown house of Dominican Friars (Blackfriars), dedicated to the Annunciation of the Blessed Virgin Mary, is said to have been founded, at some time between 1265 and 1290, by Derbhforgaill or Dervorguilla (c.1215-90), daughter of Alan (d. 1234), last king, or Lord, of Galloway. If in fact Kerenwanach belonged to this friary, the singular, 'monk', perhaps refers to the prior.

Names in *ceathramh* appear only in the more northerly parts of the Machers and in the Moors. The estates of the bishops and canons of Whithorn lay for the most part to the south (Oram 2005) and it seems likely that their officials made no use of the system in the administration of their estates, and that *ceathramh* was commemorated in place-names only outside their immediate sphere of influence. In the immediate neighbourhood of Whithorn a single trace survives. The four Outons (see chapter 2) are described in a charter of 1325 (*RMS*, i, App.1, 20) as *quatuor quarterias terre de Oton in Farinys*, 'four quarter[-lands] of the lands of Outon in Farines' – **Corwar Outon**, **Chapel Outon**, **Gallows Outon** and **Burgess Outon**, that is to say, the four together constituting one davach or ounce-land. Recollection of the assessment persisted until 1325, but left no distinctive onomastic trace. In the feu charter of 1569, already mentioned, no trace of the *ceathramh* survives.

It should be noted, in addition, that **Penkiln** and **Rispain**, the two reasonably certain *peighinn*-names, both occur well within the Whithorn sphere of influence.

(c)) *baile*

Yet another word meaning 'fermtoun' is *baile*. The basic meaning is 'place, piece of land (belonging to one family, group or individual)', only by later extension, 'homestead, farmstead, fermtoun'. As was noted in MacQueen 2002, 72, in Ireland there is no evidence for its use in place-names before the middle of the twelfth century. Much the same appears to be true of the Isle of Man, and there is no reason to suppose that things were different in Galloway or Scotland generally. *Baile* seems to have become part of the language of feudalisation, serving as a vernacular equivalent of charter-Latin *villa*, which it somewhat resembles in pronunciation. In what follows, names in *baile* are arranged by parish, starting in the north and moving southwards.

Penninghame

Balcullendoch, 322764, is, as has already been mentioned, 'fermtoun of the holly-davoch'.

Baltersan, 424615, Pont, *Baltersan*, appears to be *baile tarsainn*, 'transverse, oblique fermtoun', possibly 'fermtoun of the crossing'; cf.

Kiltersan below, chapter 4. Maxwell translates 'the house or farm at the crossing', and adds 'It is close to a former ferry or ford across the Cree'. He refers, probably, to **Carty Port**, 432625, a mile or so away, on the Cree. A minor road crosses the A714 at **Baltersan Cross**, 422621, and continues to Carty Port. Maxwell goes on, however, with a reference to Ballaterson, which occurs four times as a *treen* name in the Isle of Man (Marown, Maughold, German, Ballaugh), on which Kneen (Kneen 1925, 156) has this to say: 'It may be doubted that this signification' (i.e., 'transverse, oblique fermtoun') 'is applicable to any of them'. He proposes instead 'Irish *trosdan* or *trosnan*, "a crutch or staff," Scottish Gaelic *trasdan* or *trosdan*, "a crutch or crosier", adding that 'the four treens called Ballaterson all adjoin ecclesiastical lands ... A.W. Moore ('Manx Names') says: "The service on which these lands were held was probably that of the presentation of a staff or crosier, which the proprietors had to produce for the annual procession on the day of the saint to whom the parish church was dedicated."' Maxwell notes that **Baltersan** is near **Clary**, 424604, habitation, 'formerly the Bishop of Galloway's palace'. It is also close to **Penninghame clachan**, 413613, habitation, the site of the original Penninghame parish church.

The second element in the name Ballytrustan, Co. Down, has in the past been derived from *trosdan*, 'crutch, staff'. The most recent study, however, finds an origin in the Old Norse personal name *Thorsteinn*, Old English *Thurstan* (Hughes and Hannan 1992, 56). If this applies to **Baltersan** also, it probably indicates the presence of the *Gall-Ghaidhil*; see below, chapter 4.

Kirkcowan

Balminnoch, 272654, habitation, Pont, *Balmeanach*; *Inq. ad Cap.*, 1625, *Balmanacht*, also in **Balminnoch Wood**, 267652, represent *baile meadhonach*, 'middle fermtoun'. The lands are on the north bank of **Loch Heron**, 272648, Pont, *Herron Loch*, midmost of the Three Lochs, the other members of which are **Loch Ronald**, 265643, Pont *L. Ronald*, to the south-west, and the **Black Loch**, 279655, Pont *Loch Drein*, to the north-east.

Loch Heron is presumably 'loch frequented by heron'; the second element in **Loch Ronald** is the Norse name *Ragnald, Rögnvaldr*, borrowed as Gaelic *Raonull*; that of Pont's ***Loch Drein***, Gaelic *droigheann*, plural *droighne*, 'thorn, bramble'; 'brambly loch', 'loch around which brambles grow'.

Baltorrens, 313664, is not nowadays a farm-name, but is attached to a hill, 102 m. high, eight miles south of the Carrick border. The name may mean 'fermtoun occupied by someone called Torrance' or 'by Torrances'. The sixteenth-century spelling is *Torrens*; see, e.g., *RMS* iii, 1301, 20 August 1533. The surname is itself derived from the village-name *Torrance*, found once in Stirlingshire, south of the Kilsyth Hills, and once in Lanarkshire, near East Kilbride. The etymology is obscure. Joyce 1913 gives several examples of names in *Tooreen-*, from *tuairín*, 'grassy plot, patch of lea', a diminutive of *tuar*, 'dung, manured land'. There is at least one, admittedly minor, example of the plural, *na tuaríní*, in Seskinane parish, Co. Waterford, translated by Power (Power 1952, 171) as 'The little Cattle-Fields'. Such a plural might lead to a later Anglicised form, with added plural *-s*. Power (p.190) remarks: '*Tuar* and its diminutive ... are of very frequent occurrence in place-names throughout Waterford. They occur most frequently in mountain districts ... The word has fallen out of use in Waterford otherwise than as a component of place names. O'Donovan in at least one instance explains it as "a green grassy patch on a mountain side" such as [the] presence of a spring would produce, and this or some such meaning the word must have in many instances'. The greater number of the examples given by Power are of the simplex *tuairín*, but in Joyce the word is always first element in a compound.

Neither the word *tuar* in the sense 'dung, manured land' nor the diminutive *tuairín* exist in Scottish Gaelic. Nevertheless, 'fermtoun of the green grassy patches on a hillside' is entirely appropriate for **Baltorrens**, perhaps also for the two Torrances. It should be noted, however, that *tuairín* as a place-name element seems to be confined to the extreme south of Ireland, in terms of Wigtownshire and Scotland a remote area, not particularly likely to have extended its influence so far. It is safest to assume no more than that Torrance, a personal name, forms the second element of **Baltorrens**. If, as seems likely, the Torrances were incomers from Lanarkshire or Ayrshire, it would be the more likely that their

Baldoon ('fermtoun with a fort') Castle with modern farm building to right.

unfamiliar name would become attached to the fermtoun they cultivated.

Wigtown

Maxwell's ***Balmeg*** represents the modern **Torhousemuir House**, 394568. It is probably *baile meóig*, 'whey fermtoun'. Whey, a by-product of the manufacture of cheese, was in demand on fast-days and during Lent and Advent. Maxwell's suggestion that the name represents *baile m-beag*, 'little fermtoun', with *m-* eclipsing *b-*, is untenable.

Mochrum

I have not been able to identify Maxwell's ***Ballymellan***, perhaps *baile nam meallan*, 'fermtoun of the knolls, little hills'. Maxwell's *baile muileain* [*sic*], 'mill house or croft', is unlikely.

Kirkinner

Baldoon, *Baldone* (*RMS* iii, 1365, 17 February 1534), Pont *Baldun*, survives as **Baldoon Mains,** 425536, habitation, **West Mains of Baldoon**, 429527, habitation, **East Mains of Baldoon**, 434527, habitation, **Moorpark of Baldoon**, 418533, habitation, **Baldoon Hill**, 425534, 47 m.; also in **Baldoon Airfield** and the extensive **Baldoon Sands** of Wigtown Bay. The original holding was obviously extensive. The second element is *dùn*, genitive *dùin*, 'fort, castle', referring to the now ruined castle of the Dunbars on **Baldoon Mains** or to its predecessor. The castle was the scene of the death of Janet Dalrymple, eldest daughter of the great Viscount Stair, the story of whose marriage to Sir David Dunbar was later transformed by Walter Scott into the tragedy of *The Bride of Lammermuir*.

Balfern, *Balfarne* (*RMS* iii, 2819; 23 October 1542), survives in **North Balfern Holdings**, 437511, habitation, **North Balfern Wood**, 429505, **South Balfern Holdings**, 444508, habitation, and **Balfern Hill**, 441502, 42 m., again marking an extensive original holding. The second element is *feàrna*, 'alder'; *baile nam feàrna*, 'fermtoun of the alders'.

Ballaird, 366545, habitation, Pont *Balard*, is *baile* [*an*] *áirde*, 'fermtoun of the height, high fermtoun'. It stands at a modest elevation on the right bank of the Bladnoch.

Sorbie

Baltier, 465429, habitation, Pont *Bantyre*, is probably 'Macintyre's fermtoun'. '*Mac-*' is dropped and the surname becomes Tier in Wigtownshire, as sometimes elsewhere; cf. 'Duncan M'Olcallum and others of Clan Teir', mentioned in Black 1946, 519. See also below, chapter 4.

Balsier, 434461, habitation, Pont *Balsyir*, is also found in **Little Balsier**, 435439, and **Balsier Bridge**, 434458. It represents *baile siar*, 'fermtoun to the west', perhaps in relation not so much to the modern **Sorbie** as to the much older **Sorbie Tower**. Cf. the lost Balshere, Kirkmaiden, in the Rhinns.

Glasserton

Balcraig, Pont, *Balkraig*, has been divided to give **Big Balcraig**, 381438, habitation, and **Balcraig Moor**, 377452, habitation. The name represents *baile a' chreige*, 'fermtoun of the rock, crag', or *baile nan creagan*, 'fermtoun of the rocks'.

Whithorn

Bailiewhir, 429421, habitation, Pont *Balwhyr*, is *baile a' choire*, 'fermtoun of the vat, cauldron', presumably with reference to ***Loch of Apleby*** (Appleby), now drained. Pont places the fermtoun on the north bank of the loch. There is probably some confusion between *coire* and Irish *corr*, a feminine noun meaning 'pool, hollow containing water'. Cf. Balwherrie, 018658, Kirkcolm, in the Rhinns.

The modern spelling of the first element is a playful adaptation of the word *Bailie*, *Baillie*, 'magistrate in a burgh'. Perhaps the property was once farmed by a Whithorn baillie. Whithorn became a burgh of barony in 1459 and a royal burgh in 1511.

Balcray, **High**, 452385, habitation, and **Low**, 455381, habitation, on either side of the curiously named **Mother (Mither) Water**, may represent *baile na crè*, ‘clay fermtoun’. **Mother Water** may take its name from the fact that it supplied mill-dams along its course.

Balnab, 464398, habitation, Pont **Balnab**, is *baile an aba*, ‘fermtoun of the abbot’. The place belonged to the abbots of Saulseat (Inch), like Whithorn a Premonstratensian house; cf. another Balnab, 124609, Inch, habitation, the property of the same abbots.

Maxwell erroneously comments that the Whithorn **Balnab** ‘bears a name of very high antiquity, for Whithorn ceased to be an abbacy about A.D. 800, when the succession of Saxon abbots ended; and when the see of Candida Casa was restored in the twelfth century, the monastery was constituted a priory’. Nicolaisen (1976, 133) concurs: ‘Balnab, therefore, may well be one of the earliest *baile*-names in the south of Scotland, dating back to the eighth century’. The argument is based on two misconceptions, first, that Saxon Whithorn was governed by abbots rather than bishops; second, that the fermtoun belonged to these ‘abbots’ of Whithorn rather than to those of Saulseat. At earliest, the name belongs to the twelfth century.

Balsmith, 465394, habitation, *Balsmyth* (*RMS* iv, 2823; 1 January 1579), ‘Smith’s fermtoun’, is self-evidently late. The original Smith or Smiths may have been Lowland Scots or English incomers.

There are 18 *baile*-names in the Moors and Machars, compared to 18 in the Rhinns and Luce valley, a level balance, somewhat unexpected. Some names are common to both. In the Moors and Machars the majority are found in areas where the priory of Whithorn held a major influence, the parishes, that is to say, of Whithorn, Glasserton, Sorbie and Kirkinner. Probably of some importance here is the influence of Whithorn, as, further west, of Saulseat and Glenluce.

(d) *àirigh.*

The outfield of the fermtoun, usually on higher ground, was used to pasture and milk cattle, particularly during the season of growth and harvest. As in many other parts of the world, transhumance was practised.

At the beginning of the growing season the women and children of the community moved with the livestock to higher ground, where they lived in shielings and tended the cattle until harvest was over. A specialized vocabulary developed for this way of life. In western Scotland àirigh became the standard term for 'shieling'. There is some slight suggestion that this usage already existed in Old Irish, although the dominant sense was 'place for milking cows'; see the entry under *áirge* in the Royal Irish Academy *Dictionary of the Irish Language* (*DIL*). In Ireland *buaile*, with root-meaning 'cow-house, byre', became standard, while the corresponding term in Gaelic-speaking eastern Scotland became *ruighe* , from Old Irish *rige*, literally 'act of stretching', later 'outstretched part or base of a mountain'. In general, Galloway followed the Western Scotland usage.

Irish *buaile* appears twice in Wigtownshire, however, possibly with the meaning 'shieling'. **Shanvolley Hill**, 276625, Kirkcowan, 92 m., is *sean-bhuaile*, 'old shieling'. Maxwell gives a Lagniebole, *lag na buaile*, 'hollow of the shieling' in New Luce parish, a place which I have not been able to identify. In Gaelic *buaile* usually means 'sheep-' or 'cattle-fold' and, although the word is rare in Scottish place-names, this may also be the case here. In **Shanvolley** the adjective *sean*, 'old', may be significant in terms of the meaning.

In the Moors and Machers, the simplex *àirigh* appears several times, usually in the form *Airies*, with English *–s* added, perhaps suggesting an original Gaelic plural *àirighean*, 'shielings'. **Airies**, 275763, habitation, **High Airies**, 265671, habitation, and **Low Airies**, 260665, habitation, are in Kirkcowan parish. **Airies Hill**, 403484, 67 m., **Airies Mill Hill**, 411481, 63 m., **Over Airies,** 398482, habitation, **Little Airies**, 419481, habitation, and **Little Airies Hill**, 418482, 70 m., are all in Kirkinner parish; **Aries Knowe**, 401448, habitation, is in Glasserton Parish. The first element in **Millairies**, 418481, Kirkinner, habitation, is probably English 'mill'; it is in the immediate vicinity of **Airies Mill Hill**, 410480, 63 m., and **Mill Hill**, 414477, 65 m.

The word also occurs in compound. In **Airieglasson**, 241712, Kirkcowan, 217 m., for instance, the second element is *glas-eun*, 'grey/green bird', a name used of several small birds, rock-pipit, tree-sparrow, and sedge-warbler: the meaning is 'shieling where such small birds abound'.

Airylick, 'stony shieling'

Airyewn, 223755, Kirkcowan, habitation, is *àirigh* [*nan*] *eun*, 'bird-shieling'.

Airriequillart, 351522, Mochrum, habitation, Pont *Arychollart*, is *àirigh a' choilleir*, 'woodcutter's shieling'.

Airieolland, 308475, Mochrum, habitation, is '[St] Faolan's shieling', and is probably to be associated with the church at Kilfillan, 204546, Old Luce (MacQueen 2002, 39).

Airylick, 312493, Mochrum, habitation, is *àirigh* [*na*] *lice*, 'shieling of the flagstone' or 'shieling of the summit'. The modern farm stands on a steep and stony slope, close to the ascent of **Changue Fell**, 305495, 185 m. In poetry at least *leac* may have the sense 'hill, declivity, summit'. Airylick appears as *Arlik* in a charter dated 1st October 1545 (*RMS*, iii, 3163).

Airyligg, 254626, Kirkcowan, habitation, has the same etymology, 'shieling of the flagstone'.

Airiehassen, 372466, Kirkinner, habitation, is *àirigh a' chasain*, 'shieling of the road', probably so called from the medieval ancestor of the roads (B7021, B7085) which today link **Myrton**, ultimately **Whithorn**, and **Wigtown** by way of **Whauphill**. The B7085 passes directly in front of the modern farm.

Maxwell interprets **Garrarie**, 381400, Glasserton, habitation, as '*Gar airidh*, the near shieling or hill pasture'. *Garr-*, that is to say, he associates with *gar*, 'near', a word which 'is occasionally employed to form names' (Joyce 1871, 446). More probably the first element is the adjective *garbh*, 'rough'; *garbh àirigh*, 'rough, uneven shieling', an etymology supported by the early forms *Garwerire*, *Garowzery*, *Garwery* (*RMS*, ii, 2390, 2551, 3042, dated 8 March 1498, 22 October 1500, 30 January 1507 respectively). The *-w-* of the charter forms represents the *-bh* in *garbh*. The other names in these charters belong for the most part to the lands of **Craighlaw** in Kirkcowan parish, but 2390 makes it clear that some of the lands of **Longcastle,** 394468, on the border between Kirkinner and Glasserton parishes, were included. Garrarie, nevertheless, is some distance from Longcastle, and it remains a possibility that there were two places with the same name.

Craigairie, 244736 Kirkcowan, ?habitation, under **Craig Airie**

Fell, 235748, 320 m., the highest point in Wigtownshire, represents *creag [na h-]airighe*, 'rock of the shieling'. Pont has a *Krageri* (not identified), with the same etymology, but apparently in Glasserton parish. It is perhaps to be associated with **Garrarie** above.

Two names which might be supposed to have *àirigh* as first element, but which in fact do not, are **Airlies**, 370517, Kirkinner, habitation, Pont *Airlyis*, and **Airlour**, 346429, Mochrum, habitation, Pont *Arlair*. In both it is the first syllable which takes the stress, something which by itself is enough to rule them out as *àirigh*-compounds. There is some resemblance between Airlies and the widely-spread English Arley, OE *earn-leah*, 'eagle wood', but this does not seem a likely parallel, particularly when the form of the Wigtownshire name is plural. Airlies was one of three fermtouns in Kirkinner parish – the others were **Culmalzie,** 373532, habitation, and **Barvernochan**, 387524, habitation – granted to the prior and canons of Whithorn at some time later than the 1325 charter (*RMS* i, Appendix 1, 20, 275) but earlier than the 1569 feu charter (*RMS* iv, 2823). Airlies may in fact represent the Middle Scots word *arlis* or *airlis*, 'earnest-money', implying that the fermtoun was a preliminary gift, given in earnest of more to come, the lands, namely, of Culmalzie and Barvernochan. This cannot, of course, be proved, but seems a possible solution.

Maxwell may be right in his suggestion that **Airlour**, with stress on the first syllable, is Gaelic *ùrlar*, 'floor, flat piece of land resembling a floor', rather than a compound of *àirigh*. Several Irish parallels are listed by Joyce (1871, 425).

Norse settlers in north-west England and Yorkshire introduced the word *erg*, borrowed from Gaelic *àirigh*, and meaning 'shieling'. This is the more remarkable in that they already had a native word for 'shieling', *sætr*, found in such place-names as Satterthwaite (Lancashire), 'clearing by a shieling'. The name **Arrow**, **High** and **Low**, 446361, 453365, Glasserton, habitations, provides a likely Scottish instance of *erg*; compare Arrowe (Cheshire) and Arras, with English plural *–s*, in Yorkshire, East Riding.

(e) *carraig, sliabh.*

Long ago (MacQueen 1955) I put forward the idea that the general Scottish distribution of names with 'Carrick', *carraig*, 'rock jutting into the sea, fishing-station', and 'Slew', *sliabh*, 'hill', as the initial, defining element, suggests that these names indicate early settlement in the Rhinns by Gaelic-speakers – settlement, that is to say, well before the arrival of the Angles (7th century), or the Norse (10th century). The names indicate natural features of importance for early settlement-patterns. Subsequent discussion has been restricted to *sliabh*. W.F.H. Nicolaisen (Nicolaisen 1965) accepted it as an indicator of early settlement, but in two important articles (Taylor 2002; Taylor 2007) Simon Taylor has questioned its relevance. The methodology of his objections, however, is defective, failing, as it does, to make any distinction between *sliabh* as a defining and as a qualifying element, and discounting the very high density of *sliabh*-names in the small area of the Rhinns. I do not think that his conclusions can be accepted. The settlement, it is fairly clear, resembled that found elsewhere in Roman and sub-Roman Britain, with Irish settlers showing a marked preference for a peninsular site, as they did, on a larger scale, in Argyll and in the Lleyn and Pembrokeshire peninsulas of Wales. Charles Thomas has made the general point that in western Britain Irish settlers may well have been numerically as great in the fifth and sixth century as Germanic peoples in the south and east (Thomas 1971, 66). In the Rhinns, names in *sliabh*- and *carraig*- probably indicate the arrival of fishermen and small farmers from Ireland during the period from the fourth to the sixth centuries. The settlement was lasting, with the consequence that such names continued in fashion for a longer period.

Parallels are notably scarce in the Moors and Machers. There is only one reasonably certain example of *carraig*-. **Carrickaboys**, 488376, Whithorn, a rocky point to the north of Stein Head and Isle of Whithorn, may be a reflex of Gaelic *carraigean b[h]uidhe*, 'yellow rocks', a plural formation with English plural *–s* subsequently appended. Alternatively, it may be *carraig a' b*[*h*]*uis*, 'rock, fishing-station of the snout', with the second element the noun *bus*, genitive *buis*, 'mouth, lip, snout', a name based on some fancied resemblance of the rocks to a human or animal feature.

A little further north is **Portyerrock**, 477388, Whithorn, habitation, in a charter dated 1st January 1579 (*RMS*, iv, 2823) *Portcarrik*, i.e. *port*

[*na*] *carraige*, 'harbour of the fishing-station', with the modern **Shaddock Point**, 479390, probably the fishing-station in question. Here, however, *carraig* is in qualifying rather than defining position.

A rather less certain example is **Carghidown,** 434350, Whithorn, on the Luce Bay coast, perhaps *carraig an duin*, 'rock of the fort', with reference to **Carghidown Castle,** 434351, an Iron Age archaeological site on the top of the escarpment behind the rock. The rock originally took its name from the Iron Age site, but now the situation is reversed.

The element *sliabh*, so common in the Rhinns, occurs once only in **Sloehabbert** (400503; Kirkinner), in Pont's Atlas *Sleuhibbert*, indicating *sliabh* [*na*] *h-iobairte*, 'hill of the offering, sacrifice'. The Old Irish form of the second element is the verbal noun *idbart* or *edbart*, 'act of offering, sacrifice', used particularly of the sacrifice of the Mass, but also of any offering or presentation for a religious purpose. The name probably means 'hill where an open-air Mass was (regularly) celebrated', with the alternative possibility 'hill granted as an offering', perhaps to the parish church of Kirkinner, some two miles distant. It should be added that the position of the modern farm is not strikingly on a hill; it may be that the name once referred to an area of land around the nearby **Whaup Hill**, 403493, 73 m., land which once included the modern farm.

The simplex *iobairt* is on record in several midland-Scottish place-names. At least two, Ibert near Killearn in Stirlingshire and Ibert, near Monzie, north of Crieff, Perthshire, have survived to appear on modern maps. Watson appears to have had personal knowledge of '*Clach na h-Iobairt*, "the stone of the offering", behind Bridge of Tilt Hotel' (Watson 1926, 310), near Blair Atholl, Perthshire.

The second element in Sloehabbert has a more complex referent than in the *sliabh-* names of the Rhinns, where the second element usually indicates the dominant colour of the hill in question, or the plants which grew on it. This may suggest that Sloehabbert is a later formation, something also suggested by the general distribution of *iobairt*-names on the Scottish mainland, not in areas of primary Gaelic settlement, but rather in places where Gaelic displaced another language, usually Pictish, in the ninth or tenth-century.

One should perhaps add the possibility that the second element is

Sloehabbert — 'hill of the offering, sacrifice' : perhaps 'hill of the well'

not, in fact, *iobairt*, but *tiobairt*, ‘well, spring’, with lenition of initial *t-* after an oblique case of *sliabh*. The name would then mean ‘hill with a well or spring’.

In the Rhinns the conjunction of the names Kildonan and Slewdonan, ‘church’ and ‘hill’ of St Donan, (Kirkmaiden) suggests that sometimes at least *sliabh* was used to indicate summer-pasture for cattle and sheep moved to higher land to avoid damage to growing crops. The priest’s crops were grown around his church; his cattle grazed and were milked on the higher ground to the west. Here the use of *sliabh* comes close to that of *àirigh* elsewhere; compare Kilfillan, ‘church of Faolàn’, (Old Luce) in relation to Airyolland, ‘shieling of Faolàn’, which occurs twice, in the parishes of New Luce and Mochrum. At one time I would have said that Slewintoo (Leswalt), which I took to be *sliabh na tuatha*, ‘hill of the tenantry, peasantry’, was another example; now however I suspect that the true etymology may be *sliabh an t-samhaigh*, ‘hill of the sorrel’, with *t-* eclipsing *s-* after the definite article in the genitive singular masculine; cf. in Ireland Illaunatoo (Co. Clare) and Knockatoo (Co. Galway). This interpretation fits better with that of other Rhinns names in *sliabh*. It may nonetheless be true that *sliabh-* in Wigtownshire generally indicates summer-pasture on higher ground. The meaning of **Sloehabbert** would thus be ‘summer-pasture on which Mass is celebrated’ or alternatively ‘summer-pasture presented [to the church of Kirkinner]’.

As has been noted, the Gaelic term used for ‘shieling’ varies from one locality to another. The existence of these variant forms opens the possibility that, for a comparatively short time and in a limited area, another term, *sliabh*, may also have been used. In the Rhinns, as distinct from the Luce valley, the single instance of *àirigh* is Airies (Kirkcolm). In the Moors and Machars, the single instance of *sliabh* is **Sloehabbert**. The lack of *àirigh* names in the former and of *sliabh*-names in the latter area may indicate that when Gaelic first reached the Moors and Machers, the sense ‘summer-pasture’ for *sliabh* had disappeared, or was in the process of disappearing, replaced by the newer term *àirigh*, which perhaps reflects the arrival of the *Gall-Gháidhil*, ‘foreign (i.e., Norse) Gaelic-speakers’, who gave Galloway its modern name (MacQueen 2002, 56-8). Certainly the distribution of names in *àirigh* and its derivative *erg* corresponds remarkably with the area in which the *Gall-Gháidhil* are supposed to have been active.

In general, these Gaelic habitation-names in the Moors and Machars appear to be slightly younger than those of the Rhinns and Luce Valley. The oldest are probably more or less coeval with the oldest Anglian names; many are substantially later.

Chapter 4

Early Church Terms

(a) Annat: *annóid*

In Ireland the term *annóid*, 'foundation church', 'mother church', retains much of the sense of the Old Irish *andóit*, 'ancient foundation, church having a special connection with a patron saint, and from which others have been founded'. The ultimate derivation is from Latin *antiquitas*, 'ancient time, antiquity'. The word does not seem to have been used in the formation of place-names. The Scottish Gaelic equivalent, *annaid*, is, by contrast, relatively frequent in place-names (Watson 1926, 250-54; MacDonald 1973; Clancy 1995). Watson comments: 'our Annats are numerous, but as a rule they appear to have been places of no particular importance' (p.250). Dr Clancy's article goes some way to contradict this; '*annaid*', he says, 'corresponds roughly to its early medieval Gaelic definition as the mother church of a local community ... Many uncompounded *annaid* names may indicate the locations of these early churches, while compound ones may indicate the property, burial ground or boundary of the *andóit*' (p.114).

In the Moors and Machars the word appears three times, always in connection with a natural feature rather than a farm or dwelling:

Annat Hill, 385465, 62 m., is in Kirkinner parish. The name suggests that the *annaid* was on the top of the hill, where a site labelled 'Enclosure' is marked on the OS map. There is no suggestion that this has an early Christian origin, and there is no commemoration of an early saint in the immediate neighbourhood.

Monandie Rig 245704, 192 m. (the stress in Monandie is on the second syllable) and **Monandie Burn**, are in Kirkcowan parish. Pont has *Monenduy*, apparently a fermtoun. The name represents *mon na h-annaide*, 'hill-ground of the *annaid*'. *Rig* is 'ridge'. No trace remains of the *annaid* itself.

Knockmononday, 368568, Penninghame, 37 m. (stress on the third syllable) has *cnoc*, 'hill', tautologically prefixed to *mon na h-annaide*, 'hill of the hill-ground of the *annaid*'. The modern spelling has been influenced by *Mononday*, a Scots form of the word 'Monday'. The name was probably taken to mean 'Monday hill'!

All three sites are hill-top.

MacDonald, in the article mentioned, has established the probability that *annaid*-names denote churches which had been abandoned and subsequently relocated at a different site. In my book *St Nynia* (MacQueen 2005, 154) I suggest that in Wigtownshire such names may indicate the earlier existence of British (Welsh) churches with names in *-egles-* (*ecclesia*), of which no examples now survive in the Moors and Machars.

(b) Kil-: *cill-*.

In place-names the usual Gaelic term for a church is *cill*, locative of *ceall*, borrowed from Latin *cella*, 'monastic cell'. On modern maps and documents it appears as *Kil-*, usually followed by the name of an Irish saint of the period before the Viking incursions from Scandinavia, before about 800 AD, that is to say. Occasionally Kil- is followed by a descriptive word or phrase, but names of this kind are more common in Ireland than in Scotland. Examples of the former type include such familiar names as Kilmarnock, Kilwinning, East and West Kilbride, Kilmacolm.

For the most part, the saints commemorated lived between 500 and 700 AD; see, e.g., Watson 1926, 338. In Scotland names in *Kil-* are found, for the most part, in Argyll, Dumbartonshire, Renfrewshire, Ayrshire and Wigtownshire. In other parts of Scotland they are more sporadic. They are completely absent in Harris, Lewis, Orkney, Shetland, the north, and much of the east coast. The distribution suggests that '*Kil-* names in the northern half of Scotland, like their counterparts in the south, are in general not likely to be much younger than 800' (Nicolaisen 1976, 143). In other words, they are likely to have come into existence before 800. Most, I conjecture, belong to the period 550-750.

What the names presuppose is a small wooden church with a thatched roof, surrounded by the huts in which the members of the community lived, and by a boundary dyke or rampart made of turf.

The location was often remote. The primary aim of the members of the community was to emulate the austere life-style of the Desert Fathers of Egypt and Syria, established in western Europe primarily by the work of St Martin of Tours (d. 397).

The fact that a name commemorates a particular saint implies only that the founder of the church had a particular devotion to that saint; he may himself have been a disciple on pilgrimage or a local figure who had perhaps been healed, or thought he had been healed, by a relic of the saint, or who simply knew him/her by reputation. The saint is sometimes well-known, but often someone relatively obscure.

As noted, *Kil-* may be followed by a descriptive word or phrase. Although possible examples occur in the Moors and Machars, it is difficult to put forward any single one with confidence. There are great possibilities of confusion with names in *cùil*, 'corner, neuk', in *coille*, Irish *coill*, earlier *cael*, 'wood, forest, grove', in *ceann*, 'head' or *caol*, 'narrow', even in *ceathramh*, 'quarter-land', any of which may give rise to *Kil-* in modern orthography. Every example must be judged on its own merits. Archaeology is of no great help. Churches were constructed of flimsy material not likely to leave much of a permanent impression and any trace might well be obliterated by the fermtoun which often grew up on what had originally been an ecclesiastical site.

One possibility is **Kilsture**, 441484, Sorbie, former habitation. The site is now under forest, but the name is preserved in **Little Kilsture**, 433482, **Kilsture Forest** and **Kilsture Hill**, 444491, 53 m. Early forms are *Kelinsture* (*RMS* i, 101; reign of Robert I, Bruce), *Kilstuyre* (*RMS* ii, 2056, 9 September 1491), *Kilsture* (*RMS* ii, 2487, 24 April 1499). The second element is probably *stùrr*, 'rugged point of a rock or hill', perhaps referring to Kilsture Hill. The oldest form, *Kelinsture*, suggests that the first element is more likely to be *coill* or *coille* than *cill*; *coill an stùrra*, 'wood of the rugged point'.

Kilgallioch, 228719, Kirkcowan, above the east bank of the Tarf, is also now under forest. Pont gives *Kilgaillack*; *Inq. ad Cap.*, 1600, has *Cullingalloch*. Maxwell suggests as the derivation of the second element *gallach*, 'abounding in standing stones', an adjective formed from *gall*, 'pillar-stone, standing stone'. Joyce (Joyce 1870, 331-2) is the sole authority for this adjective, which does not appear in the dictionaries, but is preserved in the place-name Gallagh, 'scattered through all the provinces [of Ireland] except Munster', and Gallow, 'the name of a parish in Meath'. These names illustrate that the adjective might also act as a noun meaning 'place abounding in standing stones'.

The form quoted from *Inq. ad Cap.* suggests that in Kilgallioch the first element is *cùil*, 'corner, neuk', rather than *cill*. It should be noted, however, that each of the two standing stones of Laggangarn, 222717, New Luce, *lagan na gcàrn*, 'little hollow of the cairns', on the west bank of the Tarf some half-a-mile from Kilgallioch, is carved with 'a cross surrounded by four crosslets ... The rough stones seem to have been prehistoric with the carvings probably added to christianize them and to mark the ford across the river, perhaps for pilgrims coming south to Whithorn' (Murray 2006, 25). The stones are the most spectacular local monuments, but in the immediate neighbourhood of Kilgallioch there are also a number of cairns and one other possible standing stone. The area, that is to say, has many prehistoric, and therefore pagan, relics. M'Kerlie (M'Kerlie i, 622) mentions 'an old kirkyard or burial ground' in connection with the site, but nothing of the kind is recorded by the Ordnance Survey or Historic Scotland. There is at least a possibility that Kilgallioch began as a church in the immediate neighbourhood of the ford and the standing stones, perhaps with pilgrims and travellers in mind, and that one of the purposes was to make a pagan site safely Christian. The first element may well be *cill*, but no trace of the church remains.

Just possibly a similar argument might apply to **Kildarroch**. There are two places of this name. The first, *Kildarroch*, *Kildarich*, *Kildarrach* (*RMS* ii, 2390, 8 March 1498; 2551, 27 October 1500; 3042, 30January 1507), is a farm, 312623, Kirkcowan. Associated with it are **Kildarroch Wood**, another farm **Glendarroch**, 309616, and **Glendarroch Loch**.

The second, Pont *Kildarrac*, was originally a single farm, 382501, Kirkinner. It has now been divided to give **East Kildarroch** on the original site, **West Kildarroch**, 375502, **North Kildarroch**, 383507, and **South Kildarroch**, 379496. In the same neighbourhood there is also **Kildarroch Moor**, **Craigdarroch**, 376504. and **Faldarroch**, 369509.

In all these names the second element is *darach*, genitive singular of *dair*, 'an oak'. The older genitival form is *daro*. In Ireland combinations of this last with *cill* actually took place. Kildare, for instance, St Brigid's great church, is *cill daro*, 'church of the oak'. According to the *Life* of the saint by Animosus or Amchad (possibly tenth century), the place was named 'from a very high oak which Brigid loved much and blessed' (Joyce 1870, 109).

The oak was a *bile*, an 'ancient venerated tree', of the kind used in pre-Christian religious ceremonials throughout the Celtic world. It was a focus for ritual and religious awe. Brigid took advantage of this in building her church where she did. The name Kildare shows the deliberate transfer of *numen* from tree to church and from paganism to Christianity.

Is it possible that something of the same kind occurred at the two Kildarrochs? Each appears to have been named from a single oak-tree, which also provided names for other local features. Glendarroch is 'glen of the oak-tree', Craigdarroch 'rock of the oak-tree', Faldarroch '*fàl* (hedge, palisade) of the oak-tree'. The name **Knockville**, 363724, Penninghame, habitation, Pont, *Knok vill*, *cnoc a' bhile*, 'hill of the *bile*' (compare Coshieville, NN 777493, *cois a' bhile*, 'burn-foot of the *bile*' near Fortingal, Perthshire), shows that at least one *bile* was to be found in Wigtownshire, and, if one, then perhaps more.

No certainty is possible, but it is not altogether implausible that the first element of Kildarroch should be *cill*.

Kiltersan, 296619, Kirkcowan, habitation, *Kiltarsyn*, *Kiltersyn*, *Kiltersane* (*RMS* ii, 2390, 8 March 1498; 2551, 22 October 1500; 3042, 30 January 1507), the name of a farm on the flank of **Kiltersan Hill**, 296624, 137 m., looks like a compound of *cill* and *tarsuinn*, Irish *trasna*, 'transverse, oblique, lateral'. The position of the farm on the hill may explain the adjective. In Ireland, however, *Kiltrasna* is the name of two townlands, one in Co. Cavan and one is Co. Galway, each representing *coill trasna*, 'cross-wood' (Joyce 1871, 446). I suspect that this etymology also holds for Kiltersan.

Killibrakes, 311525; Mochrum, 77 m., **Killiemore House**, 354599, Penninghame, habitation, and **Killymuck** or **Killinimuck**, 323662, Penninghame, 102 m., *Kelymuk* (*RMS* iii, 1030, 22 May 1531), *Kelenemuck* (*Inq. ad Cap.*, 1633), are fairly obviously not names in

Kil-. The first element is *Killi(e)/y*-, which one might regard as most probably *coille*, 'wood, forest, grove'. Maxwell indeed takes **Killiemore**, Pont *Kaillymoir*, to be *coille mór*, 'great wood, big grove', and he is probably right. There is one slight drawback; after a feminine noun like *coille*, a following adjective is regularly lenited; *mór* ought thus to have become *mhór*, giving a modern spelling **Killievore*. Lenition however is sometimes lost in the transition of a Gaelic to a Lowland Scots place-name.

Killymuck or **Killinimuck** is straightforward; *coille nam muc*, 'swine wood'.

On the analogy of these names, **Killiebrakes** might be *coille bhreac*, 'speckled wood, grove', again with lenition of the adjective disguised, and with English plural *–s* added. Phonetically, however, the development of *breac* to *-brake* is not entirely satisfactory, and the attachment of the English plural remains unexplained. I am inclined to seek a different interpretation. Old English *bræc* (with a long vowel) means 'ground broken up for cultivation' and is found, for instance, in Breckles (Norfolk), OE *bræc-læs*, 'meadow by newly-cleared land'. The word appears in Scots as *brak*, *brack*, *brake* etc., with the meaning 'ground broken up for cultivation; a division of land under the old system of rotation of crops'. *SND* gives the following illustrative quotations: 'Such farms as are divided into 3 inclosures or, as they are commonly called, *breaks*'; 'The in-field in this county was divided into four brakes ... under the following rotation of crops'; 'In cropping it [the land] is divided for the most part into five breaks. These breaks are cultivated in regular rotation'. The word, I suggest, provides a satisfactory etymology for *–brakes*.

The preceding element, I suggest, is the intensive prefix *Killie*-, a variant form of *gillie*- and *currie*- with the general sense 'wrongly, confusedly, awry'. The meaning is thus either 'ground that has been wrongly, confusedly broken up for cultivation' or 'infield where the rotation of crops has fallen into confusion'. Under either meaning, the name is not complimentary. No modern farm stands on the site.

The second element in **Killauchie** (stress on the second syllable) **Hill**, 341621, Penninghame, 67 m., is *achadh*, 'field' – the combination of infield and outfield, that is to say, which made up a fermtoun. The most likely first element is *cùil*, 'corner, neuk': *cùil achaidh*, 'corner of the field'.

Killadam, 358563, Kirkcowan, habitation, with **Killadam Burn,** and **Killeal**, 358613, Penninghame, habitation, with **Killeal Burn**, are both obscure to me.

There are only two names directly commemorating early saints in the Moors and Machars:

Kilfillan (Sorbie), Pont *Kilphillan*, habitation, now survives in **Kilfillan Hill**, 466466, 41 m., **Kilfillan Burn** and **Kilfillan Bridge**, 468463, across the burn; *cill Fhaoláin*, 'Faolán's cell or church'. Pont gave the name to a fermtoun apparently occupying part of the site of the modern **Garlieston**, 478465, Sorbie, habitation. Cf. Airyolland above, p., and the discussion of Kilfillan, 204546, Old Luce, habitation, in MacQueen 2002, 39-40, 67.

The second is **Kilquhockadale**, 293678, Kirkcowan, habitation, *Kilquhokadaill*, RMS iv, 30, 13 November 1540; Pont *Kilquhokadaill*: *cill Choca*, 'Cuaca's cell or church', is compounded with Old Norse *dalr*, 'dale, valley'. The name as it stands is a hybrid; cf. Killernandale in Jura; also, for the process in reverse, Glenstockadale, 004615, Leswalt. The dale in question was probably that of the **Pultayan Burn**, which flows past the site.

Ainslie's 1782 map marks two sites, *Near Kilhockadale* and *Far Kilhockadale*, the first on the east, the second on the west bank of the burn.

The saint commemorated in Kilfillan is Fáelan or Faolàn, whose name means 'little wolf'. It is a hypocorism or pet form of the word *faolchú*, 'wolf'. He may be the saint whose primary connections appear to have been with Pittenweem in Fife and afterwards with Glendochart and St Fillans, Perthshire. Other commemorations are to be found in Ross-shire. He may have lived as early as the first half of the sixth century, but more probably in the early to middle eighth century. 'His cult was sufficiently important for Robert the Bruce to take his arm relic to the battle of Bannockburn and to attribute his victory to the saint's intercession' (*ODS*, 160). His crozier is now preserved in the National Museum of Antiquities, Edinburgh. His feast-day was 9 (or 19) January.

The saint appears to have been more popular in Scotland than in Ireland, where he is said to have been born; Hogan (Hogan 1910, 191) gives only a single certain, and two possible, commemorations.

Kilquhockadale, 'valley of Cuacu's cell or church'

Cuacu of **Kilquhockadale** is a woman saint, also commemorated in Kilcock (Co. Kildare), possibly also in Kilcoke (Cos. Laoighis and Tipperary). Hogan (Hogan 1910, 182) refers to 'Kilcok ... near Glenarm, Co. Antrim', which I have not been able to identify.

Joyce (Joyce 1913, 401) has this to say about her, on what authority I do not know: 'a virgin saint, also called Ercnait, foundress and patroness of Kilcock, who lived in the sixth century. She was St. Columkille's' [Columba's] 'embroiderer and was employed to make and embroider church robes and vestments'. Presumably it was Columba's monastery at Durrow, Co. Offaly, that employed her, not Iona. Her feast-day was January 8.

Pultayan in **Pultayan Burn** represents *poll taighìn*, 'burn of the little house', with reference to the original settlement, which was probably a house of women, a nunnery. The diminutive *taighin* has the same deliberately humble, early monastic overtones found in *casa*, 'cabin, hut' and *ærn*, 'shed' in Candida *Casa* and Whith*orn*.

Special mention must also be made of a saint called Màillidh, now extremely obscure, yet once widely popular. His northern commemorations are discussed in Watson 1926, 290. From Kil*mallie*, on Loch Eil in Inverness-shire, his patronage extends to the largest parish in Scotland. Glen *Mallie*, with the river *Mallie*, and Inver*mallie* at its mouth on Loch Arkaig, all take their names from him. The old name of Golspie parish in Sutherland was Kil*maly*, probably *cùil Mhàillidh*, 'Màillidh's retreat'. Dal*mally*, 'Màillidh's dale', is in Argyll. The oldest form of Inglis*maldie* on the Noran Water in Kincardineshire is *Eglis**maldiis***, 'church of Màillidh'; *eglis*, the first element, suggests that the name belongs to the early British (Welsh) rather than Irish church and that Màillidh may have been a British churchman. One might draw the same conclusion from the lost *Eglis**maldie*** or *Eglis**maly***, with the same meaning, near Burntisland in Fife.

As long ago as 1893 Sir Andrew Agnew (Agnew 1893, 123) suggested that the name Màillidh figured in a group of Wigtownshire place-names: **Water of Malzie** (Mochrum, Kirkinner), Pont, *Maille R*; **Corsemalzie**, 345523, Mochrum, habitation, Pont, *Corsmaille*; **Culmalzie**, 374532, Kirkinner, habitation, *Culmalzeoch* (*RMS* iv, 2823; 1 January

1579), Pont *Coulmaille*; **Low Malzie**, 375539, Kirkinner, habitation, and **Malzie Bridge**, 372541, Kirkinner. Maxwell cast some doubt on the suggestion, seeming to think that all the names are derived from that of the Water of Malzie (*-z-* is pronounced as *-y-*; it is in fact the old Scottish letter *yogh* rather than *-z-*), which has its source in **Fell Loch**, 308549, Mochrum, and runs for some seven miles to join the Bladnoch at 379544, Kirkinner. However, he offers no alternative etymology for Malzie.

There is, however, a clear parallel with the river Mallie in Kilmallie parish, Inverness-shire. *Allt Mhàillidh*, 'Màillidh's burn', runs into the river Orchy at Dalmally in Argyll; the name Dalmally,'Màillidh's dale', referred originally, not to the village, but to the valley of that burn.

The first element of **Corsemalzie** is Gaelic *crois*, 'cross', with the usual metathesis of the *-r-* in Scots. A wooden or stone cross may once have stood there, believed to have been erected by the saint. The name may, however, simply indicate a place where the stream was crossable on foot. The Malzie is such a small stream, and flows so slowly, that it is not, perhaps, likely that a ford would be thus singled out.

Culmalzie is *cùil Mhàillidh*, 'Màillidh's retreat', as in the old name of Golspie parish, Sutherland.

An outlying member of the group is probably Slewmallie, 127323, Kirkmaiden (Rhinns), 'Màillidh's hill'. Clachan Hill, 118320, a name indicating the former existence of a church, is nearby.

If a name in *Kil-* ever existed as a Wigtownshire commemoration of Màillidh, it has been completely lost. The same, it should be noted, is true of the neighbourhood of Dalmally and Golspie. There is also the possibility that, if the lost name once existed, it was not Gaelic in *Kil-*, but, on the analogy of *Eglismaldiis* or *Eglismaldie*, *Eglismaly*, British in *Eglis-* or *Egles-*.

(c) Kirk-

A link between speakers of Norse and Gaelic is shown by the hybrid name Kilquhockadale. The form suggests that the Gaelic element has the priority, that *cill Choca* was already in existence before the arrival of Norse-speaking settlers, who used it to give a name to the *dalr*. Following the general pattern of Norse and English names, the defining element, the name of the church, precedes the Norse generic *dalr*. In the case of Glenstockadale (Leswalt), some fifteen miles distant, the reverse is true; the name follows the Celtic pattern, with the defining element, *-stockadale*, Norse *stokka dalr*, following the generic, Gaelic *gleann*. This suggests that speakers of Norse had been established before the arrival of Gaelic speakers, who used the Norse name, *stokka dalr*, already in existence, to give a new name to the glen. The contradiction may be resolved if we assume that some Gaelic-speakers (those who gave the name *cill Choca*) had settled in Wigtownshire before any Norse settlement, but that later (?after 900) speakers of both languages arrived, probably at more or less the same time. In some groups one language predominated, in others the other. Gaelic eventually became completely dominant, but here and there in place-names traces of Norse survived, sometimes with a Gaelic overlay.

The new settlers were probably the *Gall-Ghàidhil*, 'foreign [i.e. Norse] speakers of Gaelic', who gave Galloway its modern name; see the discussion in MacQueen 2002, 49, 56-8. Their dominant language was Gaelic with a Norse admixture; possibly the commanders and administrators were Norse-speakers, who had some fluency in Gaelic. The presence of the *Gall-Ghàidhil* is most clearly indicated by names in *Kirk-*, almost certainly Old Norse *kirkja*, 'church', followed by the name of a saint, usually Irish, or by the name of Christ. The names, in other words, formally parallel those in *cill*. The generic first term is Norse, the defining second term and the form of the name as a whole is Gaelic. Usually the names are attached to places of some local importance, places, for instance, which gave their names to parishes and are still the site of the parish church. *Kirk-* may sometimes have been substituted for a name originally in *Kil-*. Despite their pagan reputation with later Irish chroniclers, the *Gall-Ghàidhil* were obviously Christian.

Kirkchrist, 362591, Penninghame, habitation, Pont *Kirk christ*, has an obvious meaning, the same as English Christchurch. This is the only Kirk-name not later attached to a parish. The name is also found in Old Luce and Kirkcudbright parishes and in the Isle of Man (Kirk Christ Lezayre and Kirk Christ Rushen). Both Manx examples are parish names.

Kirkcowan, 328606, Kirkcowan, habitation, *Kirkewane* (*RMS* ii,

1624, 16 August 1485), Pont *Kirkowan*, is probably 'church of Eoghan, Eugenius', bishop of Ardstraw, Co. Tyrone (d. 549 or 550). According to his *Life* (Heist 1965, 400-404), he was born in Ireland, but captured by pirates, who sold him into slavery in Britain, a fate from which he was rescued by Nennyo or Maucennus of the monastery of Rosnat, an alternative name for Whithorn (see chapter 2, p.. For Nennyo and Maucennus see MacQueen 2005, 146-8). Maucennus gave him a Christian education, but, together with two other youths, Tigernach and Coirpri, he was again captured by pirates and sold as a slave to the king of Gaul in Britanny. The three were set to work in a mill, but preferred to read (the Scriptures, presumably) rather than carry out their duties. After they had been punished, they fell to prayer and an angel was sent to do the work, while they continued to read. This so impressed the king that he released them and they returned to Whithorn, from which they were later despatched to Ireland. Tigernach became bishop of Clones (Co. Monaghan) and Eoghan became his coadjutor at Ardstraw (Co. Tyrone).

The *Life* of the Irish St Cainnech includes an episode (Plummer 1910, i, 160-61) in which Eoghan fights with demons in mid air, apparently above Ardstraw.

The early forms of the name strongly suggest that the saint commemorated is Eoghan. Both *–ewane* and *–owan* look like forms of that name. Maxwell does not quote these forms, but puts forward the alternative suggestion that the saint commemorated is Comhghan, brother of the matron St Kentigerna (d. 734) and uncle of Fillan. In support of this he adduces **Lincuan**, 'a pool on the river Tarf close to the old parish church (of Kirkcowan)', which he interprets as *linn Comhghain*, 'Cowan's pool'. His interpretation may well be right, but *–cuan* is probably a late formation, produced only after the *–k* of *Kirk*- had been transferred to become initial to the second part of the name Kirkcowan, a process not unusual in spoken Scots. As has been shown, there are commemorations of Fillan in Wigtownshire, but for Comhghann there is no suggestion of any such connection; he is the saint of Lochalsh in Wester Ross and of Turriff in Aberdeenshire. Eoghan's association with Whithorn is reasonably certain. Kirkcowan is a commemoration of Eoghan.

Kirkinner, 423515, Kirkinner, habitation, *ecclesiam Sancte*

Kenere de Carnesmall, 'church of St Kenera of Carnesmoel' (*RMS* i, App.1, 20, 20 May 1325; ibid. ii, 461, 17 July 1451), *Kirkynnir*, *Kirkynner*, *Kirkynnar* (*RMS* ii, 2760, 8 December 1503: iii, 1746, 3 February 1538, 3032, 15 November 1544: iv, 2866, 22 May 1579), Pont, *Kirkynnuir*, commemorates a woman saint, Cenera or Cainer, probably a disciple of Brigid, patroness of Kildare. The name is also found in *Gleann Cainneir*, now Glencannel, in Mull and in Bothkenner, Stirlingshire. A different identification is given by the lections for her *Office* in the *Aberdeen Breviary*, under 29 October. According to this, she was the daughter of a king in Orkney and became one of the eleven thousand virgin followers of St Ursula on her pilgrimage to Rome. During their attempted return she escaped the general massacre at Cologne, but was later murdered in Germany. The tale is pure fiction.

Carnesmall or **Carnesmoel** may be the original name of Kirkinner. It is probably a compound of Welsh *carn*, 'cairn, mound', with suffix *–as*, and *moel*, 'bald'. The reference is unclear.

Elsewhere I have discussed **Kirkmaiden**, 365399, Glasserton, *Kirkmidyne* (*RMS* ii, 1134, 1473), *Kirkmedin* (ibid. iii, 2944, 27 July 1543), *Kirkmadin* (ibid. iii, 3065, 10 February 1545), Pont, *Kirck maiden o the sea*, and **Kirkmadrine**, 475493, Sorbie, *Kirkmadryne* (*RMS* iv, 1436, 16 December 1562), Pont, *K mackdryn*; see MacQueen 2002, 50-54. The first is probably a commemoration of Etáin, an obscure woman saint, with mo, 'my', prefixed to the name. The identity of the saint in Kirkmadrine is uncertain. Again, *mo*, 'my', may be prefixed. The form in Pont suggests, however, that it is *mac*, 'son'.

Kirkmaiden and Kirkmadrine were both pre-Reformation parish churches.

(d) *Chapel-*

The derivation of the word 'chapel' is from Late Latin *cappella*, 'little cloak', the military cloak, that is to say, half of which St Martin of Tours cut off and gave to a beggar to cover himself during a very hard winter. The Frankish kings preserved the cloak, or part of it, as a relic in a sanctuary, known as a 'chapel', from the *cappella* enshrined there. The word then became generalised, at first applied to any such sanctified place within a church or cathedral, later to any small place of worship. The word in this generalised sense does not appear to have reached England much before the thirteenth century (see *OED*), Gaelic-speaking Ireland and Scotland only by way of English. The Gaelic spelling is *seapail.*

'Chapel-' is rare as a place-name element in Gaelic-speaking areas, and, where it does exist, is usually late. Chapel Barr, for instance, at Mid-Geanies in Ross and Cromarty, a commemoration of Barre of Cork, 'is said to have been built by Thomas MacCulloch, abbot of Fearn 1486-1516' (Watson 1926, 272-3). Such names, however, are relatively abundant in Wigtownshire. Pont's map is strewn with examples of the simplex 'Chapel'; in particular, *Chapel* is a village on one bank of what is now the Stranraer Town Burn, while Stranraer (*Stronrawyr*) stands on the other. The chapel in question was that of St John, called 'chapel' because the district round Stranraer as yet had no parish church. Both Chapel Donnan and Chapelrossan are in Kirkmaiden parish. In the Moors and Machars Maxwell gives two examples of the word in compound, **Chapelheron**, 455416, Whithorn, habitation, and **Chapel Finnian**, 279490, Mochrum. In both, as in Chapel Donnan and Chapelrossan, the word-order is Gaelic; i.e., the defining element comes first, the qualifying second. By contrast, in **Chapel Outon**, 448423, Whithorn, habitation, mentioned in chapter 2, the word-order is English or Scots with the qualifying element first, the defining second.

Chapelheron does not appear on Pont's map or on Ainslie's 1782 map; in its place Ainslie preserves three names, ***Low Chipperherrin***, ***High Chipperherrin***, and ***Chipperherrin Croft***. Maxwell gives **Chapelheron** as a variant form of ***Chipperheron***, and quotes an earlier form of the latter, *Tibertquharaine*, from *Inq.ad.Cap*. 1600. It looks as if the name **Chapelheron** came into existence only at some time after 1782, perhaps when the three ***Chipperherrins*** were amalgamated to form a single farm, and perhaps because the proprietor considered the sound of *Chipper-* in Chipperheron as too undignified for his property. He may have been influenced by the name of the nearby Chapel Outon.

Chipper- represents the feminine Gaelic noun *tiobair*, 'well' and probably indicates the existence of a holy well on the land so described.

Maxwell assumes that the second element is the name *Ciaran* (Kieran), *tiobair Chiaráin*, 'Ciaran's well'. Two well-known early Irish saints bore this name, Ciaran of Saighir, Co. Offaly and Ciaran of Clonmacnoise, also Co. Offaly. There are many other Scottish commemorations, the nearest at Kilkerran in Ayrshire. There is, I suppose, a possibility that the chapel of Chapel Outon was linked to the holy well and also commemorated Ciaran.

Ciaran of Clonmacnoise was humbly born, the son of a carpenter, and is often referred to as *mac in t-sáir*, 'the carpenter's son', modern 'Macintyre'. It may be no accident that the modern farm **Baltier**, 465429, Sorbie, '[Mac]intyre's farm', is situated less than two miles away; see above, chapter 3.

The name **Chapel Finnian** is older; it appears on Pont's map as *Chappel Finnan*. On Ainslie's map it is *Chappel Fingan ruins*. Maxwell gives *Chipperfinian* and *Chapelfinian*, thus indicating the existence of a holy well on the site. The ruins are 'of a mortared rectangular stone chapel, measuring some 6.7 m by 4.1 m internally and buttresses. It is surrounded by a drystone wall enclosing an oval area which contains a well (just inside the gate in the road wall). The chapel is named after the Celtic St. Findbar and is dated to the 10th or 11th century' (MacKie 1975, 65).

St Finbar is better known as Finnian, the hypocoristic (pet) form of the name. He is probably the scholarly bishop of Moville, Co.Down, who seems to have been trained and educated at Whithorn, and who died in 579; see *ODS*, s.v. He may have been the teacher and master of St Columba; if this is so, it establishes an interesting link between Whithorn and Iona. He is sometimes confused with Ninian himself; see MacQueen 2005, 41-4, 144-50, 152-4, 161-7.

The remains, and probably also the commemoration of Finnian, are thus early, but not very early. I suspect that the element *Chapel-* is a later introduction, a substitution for some such word as the diminutive *cillín*. The holy well probably played a major part in establishing the site as a sanctified spot. Another notable well in the neighbourhood is on the lands of **Chippermore**, 296486, Mochrum, habitation), *tiobair m[h]or*, 'big well'. **St John's Well**, 291485, Mochrum, lies to the west of the modern farm – a holy well, as the name indicates.

In Scottish Gaelic the word *clachan*, from *clach* or *cloch*, 'stone', came to mean ‘kirkton, settlement, with a small, stone-built parish church’. **Clachaneasy**, 352749, Penninghame, habitation, is *clachan Iosa*, ‘Jesus’ kirkton’, ‘Christchurch’. It is perhaps the same as Pont’s *Kerychappell*, ‘chapel quarter-land’, already mentioned in chapter 3. **Clachanlaukes**, 472350, Whithorn, a group of rocks in the sea, may have been named from a supposed resemblance to a hamlet huddling round its stone church. Alternatively, *clachan* may simply be the plural of *clach*, ‘stone’. The second element is obscure, perhaps *leac*, ‘ledge of rock jutting into the sea’, with added English plural *-s*. Compare **The Lick**, 408346, a short distance to the south.

Chapter 5

Gaelic Names – Topographic Elements

Names originally given to landscape features have sometimes become habitation-names, usually the names of farms. Frequently occurring elements are **Bar**-, Gaelic *barr*, 'top, height', usually applied to hills of modest height, **Barn**-, sometimes Gaelic *bearn*(*a*), 'gap', **Ben**-, Gaelic *beinn*, 'pinnacle, mountain, hill', **Cul**-, Gaelic *cùil*, 'nook, corner' or *cùl*, 'back', **Drum**-, Gaelic *druim*, 'back, ridge', **Glen**-, Gaelic *gleann*, 'valley', **Knock**-, Gaelic *cnoc*, 'hillock' and suffixed **-ach**, **-och**, **-ie**, indicating place. This chapter will be concerned with names involving such elements. I have tried to give complete lists in terms of geographical location.

(a) Bar-, Gaelic *barr*, 'top, height, hill'

Long ago W.J. Watson noted that 'From Cape Wrath to Loch Leven, the boundary between Argyll and Inverness-shire, the regular term for an eminence of no great height is *tulach*. South of Loch Leven *tulach* becomes rare; the term used is *barr*, "a top". In the Galloway region *tulach* is very rare, though it does occur, e.g. Fintloch for *Fionn-tulach*, "white height"; the regular term is *barr*. Here Galloway goes with Argyll' (Watson 1926, 184)

Fintloch is in the Stewartry, grid-reference 616785; cf. Marslauch, 013672, Kirkcolm, *màs-th'lach*, 'thigh hill', and Laggantalluch Head, 083362, Kirkmaiden, *leac an tulaich*, 'the stone of the hill', (for *tulach* names in the Moors and Machars see section (i) below).

Watson's position was modified by W.F.H. Nicolaisen in an article (Nicolaisen 1969, 159-66), in which he demonstrated that names in *barr* occur, not simply in Argyll and Galloway, but also in Ayrshire, Renfrewshire, Dumbartonshire, north Lanarkshire, even West Lothian, and that elsewhere in Scotland they are rare or non-existent. They also occur, in Ireland, infrequently; see for instance Baranailt, C2641, Co. Londonderry, *barr an aillt*, 'head of the glen', *Barr an Fheadáin*, 'top of the water course', the Irish name of Flagstaff, J3032, Co. Armagh, Barradashrugh,

J2518, *barr an dá shruth*, 'summit of the two rivers', and Barnamaghery, J4457, *barr na machairidhe*, 'top of the plains or farms', both these last in Co. Down (Joyce, 1913, 126-31; Ó Mainnín 1993, 126; *HDGP*, s.v.). Ireland is of course the likely ultimate source of Scottish place-names both in *barr* and in *tulach*, but in Ireland, although *barr* is much rarer than *tulach*, there is little sign of a geographic split between the two. It is difficult to explain the Scottish development.

Also to be taken into account is the existence of a Welsh cognate, *bar*, sometimes found in place-names, for instance the fairly common Bargoed, 'top of the wood'. With this should be compared Barlanark, NS 655647, LAN, a compound of Welsh *bar* and *llanerch*, 'glade', meaning 'top of the glade', a name which presumably originated in the Welsh kingdom of Strathclyde. Possibly *bar* was more favoured by the *Gwyr y Gogledd*, Men of the North, than by the people of Wales and formed a substratum to the *barr* names of SW Scotland. This, however, is only hypothesis.

Bar- sometimes occurs in habitation-names, usually farms and usually with the name also attached to a neighbouring hill. This illustrates the process known as *assart*, the transformation of rough hill-land into arable by the removal of trees, bushes and undergrowth.

As is to be expected, names in *barr* are more frequent in the Moors than in the Machars. Here I list them in order from north to south and from west to east.

Barlamachan, 327765, Penninghame, 122 m., a hill immediately south of the Cree on the Carrick border; *barr leumachan*, 'frog height', so called either because frogs were common there or from a supposed resemblance of the hill to a frog. Compare the much higher Lamachan Hill, 440772, Minigaff, KCB, 685 m. Literally, *leumachan* is 'leaper, hopper' from *leum*, 'leap, hop, jump'.

Barreid, 336765, Penninghame, a long low ridge. Etymology of second element obscure; perhaps *barr ruid*, 'penis height'. For this meaning, cf. Marslauch, 013672, Kirkcolm, mentioned above.

Barbegs, 330764, Penninghame, 118 m.: *barr beag*, 'little height', with English *-s* plural added.

Barluell, 304755, Penninghame, 143 m.: Maxwell, s.v., suggests *barr leamhchoille*, 'top of the elm-wood'. The compound second element appears otherwise only to be found in Ireland: see Hogan 1910, s.v. *lemchuill*, Joyce 1870, 491.

Barnecallagh, 254751, Kirkcowan, 166 m.: *barr nan coileach*, 'height of the cocks', probably black-cocks or grouse.

Barneconahie, 259750, Kirkcowan, 150 m.: *barr in c*(*h*) *oìnneachaidh*, 'height of the meeting, assembly'.

Barnaclagnahie, 261747, Kirkcowan, 153 m.: *barr in c*(*h*)*luicíne*, 'height of the little bell'. The reference is probably to the shape of the hill.

Barnyclagy, 295739, Penninghame, 148 m.: *barr in c*(*h*) *laigtheachan*, 'hill of the belfry-steeple', again probably with reference to the shape.

Barvalgans, 293734, Penninghame, 142 m.: *barr a' bhalgain*, 'height of the little bag, satchell', again probably with reference to the shape. English plural *-s* added.

Barlae, 299734, Penninghame, 148 m., here a hill-name, but in other parishes also a habitation-name: *barr* [*nan*] l*aogh*, 'the calves' hill'. The word *laogh* also means 'fawn, young deer', which in this situation gives perhaps a more convincing meaning.

Barchessie, 317707, Penninghame, 109 m.: *barr deise*, 'south height', in relation to **Knowe** ('knoll'), 313714, habitation, or more probably to **Beoch** (Gaelic *beitheach*, 'birch-wood'), 321716, habitation, with its motte.

Bartyke, 322676, Kirkcowan, 100 m.: second element obscure.

Barharrie, 302674, Kirkcowan, 112 m.: *barr* [*na*] *h-airighe*, 'height of the shieling' or *barr* [*na*] *h-eirbhe*, 'height of the dyke'.

Barnkirk, 307670, Kirkcowan, 107 m.: probably *barr nan cearc*, 'height of the hens'. The reference may be to partridges or other game-birds.

Bartaskie, 322670, Kirkcowan, 80 m.: *barr* [*an*] *t-asgaidh*, 'height of the boon, present'.

Barbae, 311666, Kirkcowan, 116 m.: *barr beith*, 'birch height'.

Barfad, 327665, Kirkcowan, habitation; **Barfad Loch**, 324663; **Barfad Fell**, 322656, 125 m., and **Ring of Barfad**, 333666, under

Ring Hill (Gaelic *rinn*, 'point, promontory'), 330669, 88 m.: *barr fada*, 'long height', probably referring to Barfad Fell. This is the most northerly habitation name in *barr*.

Barnkirk Hill, 394664, Penninghame, 58 m.; **North Barnkirk**, 392666, habitation, and **South Barnkirk**, 398651, habitation; Pont *Barnkerk*: see above, 307670.

Barnely Hill, 342659, Penninghame, 84 m.: *barr na h-aille*, 'height of the steep river bank'. On the east bank of the Bladnoch at its junction with the Black Burn.

Barneam Hill, 382658, Penninghame, 54 m.: may be *barr an fheuma*, 'poverty height'.

Barbuchany, 405643, Penninghame; *RMS* ii, 3018, 23 December 1506, *Barbuchane*; 3134, 16 September 1507, *Barbochany*; Pont *Barbuchanty*; also **High Barbuchany**, 398644: both names now denote habitations with no corresponding hill-name. Barbuchany is situated on the higher ground above the west bank of the Cree. It is also close to **Barrhill Farm**, 411633 below, much closer, in fact, than **Upper** or **Nether Barr**, 410629, 419636. It is thus possible that the Bar- of Barbuchany may be **Barr Hill**, 412631. The second element probably contains a reference to the district of Buchan, Aberdeenshire. The link may well be the family of the Comyn Earls of Buchan. Before 1234, Helen, daughter of Alan, last Lord of Galloway, married Roger de Quincy, Earl of Winchester (c.1195-1264). On Alan's death in 1264 the couple inherited most of what is now Wigtownshire. Their daughter Elizabeth married Alexander Comyn, 6th Earl of Buchan (d.1289), who became Sheriff of Wigtown after the death of Roger, thus gaining much influence west of the Cree. His caput was **Cruggleton Castle**, 475429. Their son, John Comyn, 7th Earl of Buchan (c.1250-1308), succeeded him as Sheriff of Wigtown in 1290. In May 1300 he came to Galloway in an attempt to win it over to the Scottish cause in the struggle against the English king, Edward I (reigned 1272-1307). In August of the same year, together with his cousin, the Red Comyn, John Comyn III, Lord of Badenoch (murdered 1306), and Sir Ingram de Umfraville, he faced Edward's forces across the Cree, somewhere near the modern Newton Stewart, only to flee when the English cavalry crossed the river. Possibly the name Barbuchany preserves some remembrance of this skirmish. It may mark the position of Buchan's forces before the encounter.

Barneight, 327640, Kirkcowan, habitation; Pont *Barnacht*: *barr an echt*, 'hill of the slaughter, murder'. The reference is obscure.

Barskeoch, 361636, Penninghame, habitation; *RMS* ii, 3042, 30 January 1507, *Bernskeach*; **Low Barskeoch**, 362633, habitations: *barr nan sgeach*, 'hawthorn height'. Both are on an unnamed hill, topped by a cairn.

Barnean, 379636, Penninghame, habitation: *barr nan eun*, 'height of the birds' or 'of the chickens'. It stands under **Drumnawantie Hill**, 375634, 83 m., *druim nam bhantaighe*, 'ridge of the housewives', possibly indicating hen-wives; cf. Hen Knowe, 093433, in the grounds of Logan House, Kirkmaiden. Barnean is close to **Merton Hall**, 382639, for which it may have provided chickens and eggs.

Bardonachie, 256635, Kirkcowan, 120 m.; Pont, *Bardonachy*: *barr Donnchaidh*, 'Duncan's height'. The name is fairly common, but possibly indicates Donnchadh mac Gillebrigte (c.1175-1250), Duncan son of Gilbert, grandson of Fergus, 1st Lord of Galloway, ousted from his share of the Lordship by his cousin Lachlann or Roland, 3rd Lord of Galloway, but created 1st Earl of Carrick in or about 1189.

Barr Hill, 412631, Penninghame, 106 m.; also habitations, **Barrhill Farm**, 411643, **Upper Barr**, 410629, **Nether Barr**, 419636, **Moor Park of Barr**, 407632; also **Barr Moor**, 412626, **Carse of Barr** (this last flood-plain almost enclosed by the Cree). Pont, *Barr* and *Barhill*: *barr*, 'top, height'. See also **Barbuchany**.

Barskeoch Fell, 297629, Kirkcowan, 177 m.; also **Barskeoch**, 296626, habitation, *RMS* ii, 3042, 30 January 1507, *Bernskeach*, and **Barskeoch Moss**, 286626: see **Barskeoch**, 361636 above. The *-n-* in *RMS* is intrusive.

Barhoise, 338619, Kirkcowan, habitation; *RMS* ii, 3042, 30 January 1507, *Barquhoise*; also **Barhoise Burn**, **Barhoise Mill**, 339616, **Barhoise Bridge** (over the Barhoise Burn), 333616, **Linn of Barhoise** (waterfall on the Bladnoch): *barr a'chois*, 'height of the hollow, cavern, recess'. Nearby is an unnamed hill, 336618, 60 m.

Barraer Fell, 373617, Penninghame, 123 m., the highest point in the neighbourhood; **Barraer**, 381619, habitation: *barr reamhar*, 'fat, big hill'.

Barwhirran, 405616, Penninghame, and **Barwhirran Cottage**, 398612, both habitations: *barr a' choirean*, 'height of the little circular hollow'. The name better fits Barwhirran Cottage under **Cauldside Hill**, 398614, 53 m., than Barwhirran itself.

Barlauchlin, 389615, Penninghame, habitation; Pont, *Barlachlen* which he places on the Bishop Burn: *barr Lachlainn*, 'Lachlan's height', or possibly 'McLachlan's height' with 'Mc-' dropped in accordance with common Galloway usage. McLachlan is still reasonably frequent as a Galloway surname. It looks, however, as if here the reference is to Lachlan, better known as Roland son of Uchtred, 3rd Lord of Galloway, who died in 1200. His Gaelic name was Lachlan, but in adult life he preferred to be known by the Norman-French Roland. His Gaelic-speaking subjects probably stuck to the original. The road from the modern Barlauchlan to **Barlauchlan Bridge**, 400613, across the Bishop Burn runs immediately to the north of **Rolland Hill**, 400610, 42 m.. This may be a 'corrected' form of the original Barlauchlan. Possibly it marks the spot where Lachlan/Roland's forces defeated the supporters of Donnchadh son of Gillebrigte after the death of Gillebrigte in 1185. See above, **Bardonachie**, 256635.

Barmore Hill, 283605, Kirkcowan, 111 m.; **Barmore**, 282611, habitation, Pont *Barmoir*; **Barmore Moss**, 282602, and **Black Hill of Barmore**, 282622, 107 m.: *barr mór*, 'big hill'.

Barlennan, 342609, Penninghame, 55 m., above the Bladnoch; **Barlennan Hill**, 321602, and **Barlennan**, 322603, habitation, both Kirkcowan, above the Tarf: *barr leànain*, 'top of the haugh'.

Barbunny, **Near**, 293608, 109 m., **Far**, 298611, 111 m., Kirkcowan; Pont, *Barbunduy*, habitation: *barr a' bunduibh*, 'height of the roots of bracken' used as thatch for houses or corn-stacks.

Barvennan, 387605, Penninghame, under **Bennan Hill**, 390604, 75 m.: *barr a' bheinnein*, 'height of the little peak'.

Barhapple Hill, 301605, 103 m.; **Barhapple**, 300602, Kirkcowan, habitation; **Barhapple Moor**, 298606: *barr a' chapuill*, 'height of the horse'.

Barchly Hill, 305595, Kirkcowan, 95 m.; **Barchly**, 305596, habitation; *Inq. ad Cap.* 1625, *Barincla*: *barr in chlaidh*, 'height of the trench', referring to the space between Barchly Hill and **Mid Hill**, 306598, 82 m..

Bartorran Hill, 329593, Kirkcowan, 60 m.: *barr torrain*, 'little-hill height'.

Bartrostan, 380593, Penningham, habitation; **Bartrostan Burn**; **Bartrostan Moss** , 380592; Pont, *Bartrostan*. Bartrostan is on **Auld Hill**, 378593, 89 m., probably the original *barr*: *barr trasdain*, 'crozier height', from a fanciful belief that the shape of Auld Hill, together with **Knockcuddie**, 378597, 88 m., *cnoc udaig*, 'woodcock hillock', resembled a bishop's or abbot's crozier.

Barquhill Hill, 333586, also 351557, Kirkcowan, 72 m., 62 m.; **Barquhill**, 353555, Kirkinner, habitation; *RMS* ii, 2521,14 February 1500, *Barquhill*; 3294, 29 January 1508, *Barquhill*; **Barquhill Burn**: *barr chuil*, 'back hill', the first in relation to **Boreland**, 352585, habitation, Pont, *Boirland of Kingston*, 'land providing supplies for a lord's table', the second to **Crouse**, 365553, probably *cruadhas, cruas,* 'hardship'; see below, p.140.

Barsallach, 451583, Penninghame, habitation; Pont Barsallach: *barr salach*, 'foul, dirty height'. It is in flat bog-country between the Bishop Burn and the Cree, with no obvious hill in the vicinity.

Barmeen Hill, 323583, Kirkcowan, 82 m.: *barr mìn*, 'smooth hill'.

Barrachan, 363576, Wigtown, habitation; Pont *Barchraichan mill*: *barr a' chreachainn*, 'height of the stony declivity of a hill'. It stands on the southern slope of **Knocknamad Hill**, 364580, 59 m., perhaps *cnoc na m-bád*, 'hillock of the boats', part of which is called **Boat Hill**. Both names probably derive from the shape of the hill.

Barflawen Hill, 357570, Kirkcowan, 52 m.: *barr a' bhlàbheinn*, 'height of the yellow peak'.

Barlae Hill, 398534, Kirkinner, 71 m.; **Little Barlae**, 395532, habitation; **Barlae**, 397531, habitation; see above, **Barlae**, 299734.

Barvernochan, 386523, Kirkinner, habitation; Pont, *Barvarrunach*: probably *barr feòir-nan-chon*, 'couch-grass height'; *barr feoirnachain*, 'height of the lesser shrew, fairy mouse' is also possible.

Barglass, 411519, Kirkinner, habitation; **Barglass Cottage**, 410522; **Barglass Bridge**, 412516, across the **Maltkiln Burn**: *barr glas*, 'green height'; perhaps from **Dam Hill**, 412514, 63 m.. The construction of the dam across the burn probably gave rise to the change of name for the hill. The dam in turn probably served **Mildriggan Mill**, 421521, Kirkinner, for which see above, chapter 2.

Barrachan Hill, 363503, Mochrum, 105 m.; **Barrachan**, 362495, habitation, *RMS* iv, 1173, 16 May 1557, *Barbrochane*, Pont, *Barchracchan*; see above **Barrachan**, 363576. The second *-b-* in the *RMS* form probably results from dittography.

Baryerrock Hill, 391503, Kirkinner, 62 m. **Baryerrock**, 389508, habitation: *barr iaraig*, 'weasel hill' or 'squirrel hill'.

Barwhanny Hill, 410496, Kirkinner, 76 m.; **Barwhanny**, 410494, habitation; *RMS* ii, 87, 18 March 1426, *Barquhonny*; 1545; 1545, 24 January 1483, *Barquhone*; 1718, 11 March 1488, *Barquhone*; 2525, 21 February 1500, *Barquhonny*; 2954, 30 March 1506, *Barquhony*; Pont, *Barwhony*; **Barwhanny Cottages**, 408494, habitation. The second element is obscure. Maxwell's *barr a' bhainne*, 'hill of the milk, milking hill' has some attraction, but *bh-* would normally give rise to *w-* or *v-*, rather than *wh-*, vouched for by the early forms. I suspect that the *RMS* references are not to this Barwhanny, but to a place in the neighbourhood of Stranraer, possibly the modern Glenwhan Hill or The Eyes, 142612, Old Luce, 49 m. Pont's reference is to the Kirkinner site.

Barhobble, 310494, Mochrum, *Chapel* on O.S. 1:25000 map; see Cormack 1995, 6: probably *barr shaipél*, 'chapel height'.

Barley Hill, 291482, Mochrum, 97 m.: see above, **Barlae**, 299734.

Barr Hill, 328471, Mochrum, 138 m.; **West Barr**, 320460, habitation; **East Barr**, 330472, habitation: *barr*, 'top, height'.

Bar Hill, 437456, Sorbie, 53 m.: *barr*, 'top, height'.

Barledziew Hill, 428455, Sorbie, 67 m.; **Barledziew**, 426450, habitation, *RMS* iv, 764, 28 February 1553, *Barlathyew*; **Low Barledziew**, 430455, habitation: *barr lèideach*, 'shaggy height'.

Barwinnock Hill, 390430, Glasserton, 75 m., **Barwinnock**, 385437, habitation; Pont *Barvannoch*: second element obscure. Maxwell's suggestion, *barrfhennoc*, 'lazybed hill', or 'crow hill', is not tenable. Aspirated *f-* is silent and would not give rise to *w-* in transcription.

Barsalloch, **North**, 346419, Mochrum, habitation, **Mid**, 353419, habitation, **South**, 356414, habitation, **North Barsalloch Cottage**, 344416, habitation, **Barsalloch Point**, 344411, natural feature: see above,

Barsallach, 451583.

Fell of Barhullion, 375418, Glasserton, 136 m., Pont, *Baryillen hill*, **Fell of Barhullion**, 375425, habitation: *barr chuilinn*, 'holly height'.

Barmeal, 383413, Glasserton, habitation: *barr maol*, 'bare, bald hill'. The farm is on a hill, otherwise unnamed, 67 m. high.

I have not been able to identify ***Barfalls***, Penninghame, ***Barallan***, Wigtown, ***Barjarg***, Kirkinner, and ***Barnagee***, Glasserton, all listed by Maxwell.

(b) Barn-, Gaelic *bearn*(*a*), 'gap'

bearn(a) signifies a gap between hills, usually with a stream running through, but with no necessary suggestion of a regular road or path. Where Gaelic has disappeared as a spoken language, as in Galloway, it is often difficult to distinguish *bearn*(*a*) from *barr*, followed by the definite article *an*. Topography offers a possible, but not wholly reliable, guide.

Names in *bearn*(*a*), like those in *barr*, have sometimes become attached to habitations.

Barnair, 340770, Penninghame, hill, 95 m., on right bank of the Cree, with White Hill, 349770, Minnigaff, 89 m. on opposite bank: probably *bearn odhar*, 'dun gap', with the name transferred to the hill.

Barney Cleary, 318752, Penninghame, hill, 127 m., immediately to the west of the narrow gap between Black Loch, 319756, and Loch Ochiltree, 316744: *bearna na cléire*, 'pass of the clergy'. On the far side of Black Loch is **Culnavie Moss**, 324757, *cùil an neimhidh*, 'neuk of the sanctuary', suggesting the former existence of a religious site in the immediate neighbourhood.

Barnsladie, 289684, Kirkcowan, a slight gap in the hills bordering the upper reaches of the **Pultayan Burn**: *bearn na slaide*, 'robbery, plunder gap'.

Barnharrow, 298664, Kirkcowan, habitation; **Rig of Barnharrow**, 300662, hillside: *bearn na h-àirighe*, 'gap of the shieling'. An unnamed small tributary of the Black Burn emerges between two unnamed hills at Barnharrow and flows under Rig ('ridge') of Barnharrow.

Barney (stress on first syllable) **Hill**, 329597, Kirkcowan, 62 m.: *bearna*, 'gap'. Refers to gap between Barney Hill and **Thorny Hill**, 327599, 64 m., or **Bartorran Hill**, 329593.

Barness (stress on second syllable), **High**, 385541, Kirkinner, habitation; **Low**, 396549, habitation; Pont, *Barness mill*: *bearn éasa*, 'waterfall gap' or 'gap of stream with high precipitous banks'. Both places are on the right bank of the Bladnoch.

Barnbarroch, 398515, Kirkinner, habitation; *RMS* ii, 2335, 17 December 1496, *Bernberach*; iv, 2665, 16 March 1577, *Barnebarroch*; Pont, *Barnbarraugh Cast*[*le*]: *bearn b*(*h*)*arraich*, 'birch gap', between **Hawk Hill**, 396515, 71 m., and **Broom Hill**, 397513, 47 m.; alternatively where the upper waters of the **Maltkin Burn** passes the ruined **Barnbarroch House**, 399514, built on the site of the ancestral home of the Vaus family.

(c) Ben-, Gaelic *beinn*, 'pinnacle', 'mountain, hill'; diminutive Bennan, *beinnean*, 'little hill'.

The word occurs in Ireland and, in Scotland, is usual in hill- and mountain-names north of the Clyde-Forth line. Ben Lomond, NS 368029, 974 m., is a familiar example. It occurs rarely in the Moors and Machars.

Benbrake Hill, 227747, Kirkcowan, 312 m.: *beinn b*[*h*]*reac*, 'speckled hill'.

Bennan of Kirkcalla, 301746, Penninghame, 166 m.

Bennylow, 303641, Kirkcowan, 167 m.: probably *beinn na làimh*, 'hill of the hand or handle', with reference to its position on **Fell End**, 307643, of which it is a spur.

Bennan Hill, 297487, Mochrum, 157 m.

Maxwell also lists ***Benbuie***, Glasserton, *beinn b*[*h*]*uidhe*, 'yellow hill', which I have not identified. He remarks 'It is a headland on the coast, and the cliff is coloured with the rich yellow of a lichen – *Parietaria*'.

(d) Craig-, Gaelic *creag*, 'rock, crag, hill'; *càrn*, 'cairn'.

Craig Airie Fell, 236736, Kirkcowan, 320m. (1051 feet, the highest point in Wigtownshire); Pont, *Hill of Kraig-ary*; **Craigairie**, 243736, habitation; Pont *Kraigary*: *creag àiridhe*, 'shieling hill'.

Craigie, 341736, Penninghame, habitation: see below, (i).

Craigmoddie, 245721, Kirkcowan, 187 m.; Pont, *Kraig maddy*: *creag m(h)adaidh*, 'dog, fox or wolf crag'.

Craigree, 306685, Kirkcowan, 123 m.: *creag fhraoich*, 'heather crag'.

Craighore, 290678, Kirkcowan, 129 m.; *creag odhar*, 'dun crag'.

Craignarbie, 296661, Kirkcowan, 139 m.: *creag na h-arpaig*, 'crag of the adder'. Maxwell suggests *creag an earba*, 'crag of the roe'.

Meikle Craig, 342572, Kirkcowan, 60 m.: *creag*, qualified by Scots *meikle*, *muckle*, 'big'.

Craigdow Moor, 33/34 56/57, Kirkcowan; **Craigdow Burn**, flowing from **Black Loch**, 329568, Mochrum, to **Clugston Loch**, , 344573, Kirkcowan; *RMS* ii, 2520, 2521, 14 February 1500; 2758, 22 March 1501, *Cragdow*, habitation; 3294, 29 January 1509, *Craigdow*, habitation: *creag d(h)ubh*, 'black crag', possibly referring to **Meikle Craig**.

Craigeach (stressed on second syllable), 391561, Mochrum, habitation; *RMS* ii, 2521, 14 February 1500, *Craghauch*; Pont, *Kraigailch*; **Craigeach Fell**, 319560, 131 m.: **Craigeach Moor**, 330560: *creag fhiach*, 'ravens' crag'.

Craiglarie Fell, 319547, Mochrum, 118 m.; **Craiglarie Moss**, 31/32 55; Pont, *Kraiglary*, habitation: *creag làireach*, 'mares' crag'; cf. the nearby **Craignagapple**.

Craignagapple, 316545, Mochrum, 95 m.: *creag na gcapull*, 'crag of the mares'.

Craigbennoch, 362515, Mochrum, habitation: *creag beannach*, 'horned, pointed crag', perhaps referring to the nearby **Tintock Hill**, 367517, 98 m.

Craigdarroch, 376504, Kirkinner: *creag daraich*, 'oak-tree crag'.

Craig, 418421, Whithorn, habitation; **Craig Cottages**, 416419, habitation: *creag*.

Craigengour, 363402, Glasserton, 52 m. (on a steep slope to Luce Bay): *creag nan gobhar*, 'crag of the goats'.

Craigdhu, 397402, Glasserton, habitation, 77m.; Pont, *Kreigdow*: *creag dhubh*, 'black crag'.

Craiglemine (accented on final syllable), 406392, Glasserton, habitation, 83 m.; **Low Craiglemine**, 399390, habitation; *RMS* iv, 2823, 1 January 1579, *Craigilmayne*: obscure. Maxwell's *creag nam meann*, 'crag of the kids', is unconvincing. **Craigle**- may be a tautological compound of Gaelic *creag* with Scots/English *hill*; cf. **Cruggleton** above, chapter 1, and probably *Knocklemine*, NW 968656, Leswalt, 73 m. A Gaelic adjective, perhaps *mìn*, 'smooth', has been added; 'smooth hill'.

Some of these 'crags' are topped by cairns, sometimes dating from the Bronze Age. The word *càrn*, 'cairn', is occasionally applied to rising ground.

Cairngapple, 329637, Kirkcowan, habitation, surrounded by low hills: *càrn na gcapull*, 'cairn of the mares'. There is no trace of a cairn in the immediate neighbourhood.

Cairn Head, 487383, Whithorn, a low promontory jutting into Wigtown Bay; **Cairnhead Mote** (archaeological site marked 'fort'), 487382; **Cairnhead**, 479382, habitation: *càrn*, together with Scots/English *head*, 'promontory'. No trace of a cairn, but the ruins of the fort may have given rise to the name.

(e) Cul-, Gaelic *cùil*, 'corner, neuk, retreat'

Initial *Cul*- is a common element in Wigtownshire place-names and usually represents Gaelic *cùil*, 'corner, neuk, retreat'; sometimes Gaelic *cùl*, 'back'. In general I take it to be the former, but the latter always remains as at least a possibility. In chapters 3 and 4 I have already mentioned several names in *Cul*-; **Culbratten**, for instance, **Culmalzie**, **Culscadden** and **Killauchie Hill**.

Culnavie in **Culnavie Moss**, 324757, Penninghame, represents *cùil an neimhidh*, 'neuk of the sanctuary'.

As noted in Chapter 4, **Killauchie**, 341621, Penninghame, is *cùil achaidh*, 'corner of the field'. Here as elsewhere *achadh* implies ‘fermtoun’. Maxwell defines the term as ‘Cullachie, Heigh and Laigh (two fields on Glasnick farm)’. **Low Glasnick,** 343618, Penninghame, and **High Glasnick,** 352625, Penninghame, Pont *Nether Glasnik* and *O*[*vir*] *Glasnick*, were separate fermtouns already by the late sixteenth century. **Low Glasnick** is closer to **Killauchie Hill** and is thus probably the *achadh* intended; alternatively the name may originate from a time when only a single fermtoun existed. **Glasnick** is probably a compound of *glas*, ‘green’, and *cnoc*, ‘hill’; the name may actually refer to **Killauchie Hill**.

Culmalzie, 374532, Kirkinner, habitation, is *cùil Màillidh*, ‘Màillidh’s retreat’. See above chapter 4.

Early forms of **Cullach**, 375653, Penninghame, *RMS* ii, 3018, 23 December 1506, *Culclachach*: 3134, 16 September 1507, the corrupt *Culeclagic*; Pont *Coulclacch* (for *Coulclacach*?), suggest *cùil c*[*h*]*lachach*, ‘stony corner’.

Culcreuchie is the original name of **Penninghame House**, 382698, Penninghame, habitation. Early forms are *Culquhreauch*, *Culcreach*, *RMS* ii, 2943, 27 February 1506: iii, 2576, 10 January 1542, Pont *Coulcreochy*. Maxwell suggests *cùil* [*na*] *croiche*, ‘gallows corner’. Penninghame House, however, stands on the right bank of the **Cree**, *abhainn na criche*, ‘boundary river’, marking the original Wigtownshire boundary. It seems probable that **Culcreuchie** is *cùil* [*na*] *criche*, ‘boundary neuk’, or even ‘Cree-side retreat’.

Culvennan, **West**, 297651, Kirkcowan, and **East**, 307655, Pont *Coulvennan*, stand to the west of **Culvennan Fell**, 311650, 213 m. The name represents *cùil a’ bheannain*, ‘neuk of the little peak’, referring to the summit of **Culvennan Fell**.

Culquhirk, 426567, Wigtown, Pont *Coulwhorck*, is *cùil a’ choirce*, ‘oat corner’, ‘corner where oats are grown’.

The second element in **Culshabbin**, 304509, Mochrum, habitation, and **Culshabbin Schoolhouse**, 307510, habitation, is *siaban*, ‘sand-drift, sea-spray, spindrift’; *cùil* [*an t-*] *siabain* is thus probably ‘spindrift neuk’. Luce Bay lies some two miles distant towards the south-west, the direction of the prevailing wind. The name implies that, probably only under extreme weather conditions, spindrift, or possibly blown sand, was funnelled up the **Alticry** glen to reach Culshabbin.

Culbae, 387490, Kirkinner, habitation, *RMS* ii, 2392; 13 March 1498, *Kulvey*, Pont *Coulbee*, is *cùil bheith*, 'birch-tree corner'. *Kulvey* preserves aspiration of *b-* in the genitive plural, lost in later forms.

Maxwell gives ***Culfad***, Kirkinner, which I have not been able to identify. The second element is the adjective *fada*, 'long, distant'.

Culgarie, 375485, Kirkinner, habitation, *RMS* ii, 2392, 13March 1498: iii, 3309, 25 August 1546, *Culgare*; Pont *Coulghary*, is probably *cùil a' ghàraidh*, from *gàradh*, 'garden', 'wall, dyke'; the meaning is 'garden neuk' or 'walled neuk'. The garden or walled space was probably for vegetables, rather than flowers or shrubs.

Culnoag, 420471, Sorbie, habitation, and **Culnoag Hill**, 421472, 64 m., *RMS* iii, 2266, 5 February 1541, *Culnook*, Pont *Coulnowack*, is perhaps *cùil na noige*, 'neuk of the anus' (*noig*, fem., 'anus'). Pont puts it at the lower end of *L*[*och*]. *Boirlant*, better known as **Dowalton Loch**, now drained. The outflow of water from the loch probably gave rise to the name.

Culderry, 475467, Sorbie, habitation, is *cùil* [*na*] *doire*, 'oak-grove corner'.

Culkae, **West**, 420456, Sorbie, habitation, and **East**, 425458, habitation, also **Culkae Hill**, 422466, and **Culkae Bridge**, 420466, *RMS* iii, 2266; 5 February 1541, *Cowlkay*, is probably *cùil a' c*[*h*]*adha*, 'neuk of the pass', possibly 'neuk of the path, road'. Gaelic *cadha* means 'pass'; the cognate Irish *caoi* means 'road'.

(f) Drum-, Gaelic *druim*, 'back, ridge'

Drum-, representing Gaelic *druim*, occurs frequently in the Moors and Machars, for the most part applied to hills the length of which considerably exceeds the breadth. These hills lie generally on a north-south axis, indicating stages in the advance, and more particularly the retreat of glaciers in the Ice Age back to their place of origin in the Merrick range. As the ice advanced, it scooped up material which later, in the course of retreat, it deposited to form the drums.

Gaelic *druim*, 'back, ridge', sometimes refers to major natural features. *Druim Albainn*, Drumalbin, for instance, is the ridge which stretches all the way up the western side of Scotland from Ben Lomond in the south to Ben Spionnaid in the north, and which marks the watershed between east and west. The Wigtownshire drums are smaller and more homely.

Drumanoon, 249757, Kirkcowan, 197 m.: *druim nan uan,* 'ridge of the lambs'.

Drumstable, 281753, Penninghame. 134 m.: *druim stàbuill*, 'stable ridge'. The ridge is on the west bank of **Loch Maberry**, and it is probable that the name was given with reference to **Loch Maberry Castle** on a small island.

Stabull is a loan-word, probably from English *stable* rather than Latin *stabulum,* the Irish derivative of which is *sabhall,* 'barn'. Drumstable is thus unlikely to be an old name; it is probably no earlier than the 12th century.

Drumdown, 245752, Kirkcowan, 183 m.; 243731, Kirkcowan, 200 m.: *druim donn*, 'brown ridge'.

Drumfort, 281747, Penninghame, 157 m.: *druim fuairid*, 'colder ridge'.

Drumaclown, 252742, Kirkcowan, 180 m.: *druim na cluaine*, 'ridge of the pasture'. There are sheepfolds on a neighbouring hill, **The Stand**, 256739, 185 m., but the ground was not invariably used for pasture. **Stand** means 'the standing place from which a hunter or sportsman may shoot game' (*OED*).

Drumdow, 275735, Penninghame, 157 m.; 298573, Kirkcowan, 82 m.; 332498, Mochrum, 87 m.; 400456, Glasserton, 66 m.: *druim dubh*, 'black ridge'.

Drummakibben, 263731, Kirkcowan, 142 m.: the second element is the surname McCubbin, variant of McGibbon, 'son of Gibbon': 'McCubbin's ridge'. 'Gibbon' is a diminutive of 'Gilbert', often used as equivalent to the Gaelic *Gille Bríghde*, 'servant of [St.] Brigid', for instance in the name of Gilbert or Gille Bríghde, second Lord of Galloway (d. 1185). It is possible, though unlikely, that the name of the ridge contains a reference to Donnchad or Duncan, latterly Earl of Carrick, son of Gille

Bríghde (d. 1250). At least it refers to someone of local importance.

Druminnarbel, 255730, Kirkcowan, 167 m.: apparently *dromannan* (plural of *druim*) *air beulaobh*, 'ridges in front', or *druman* (diminutive of *druim*) *air beulaobh*, 'little ridge in front'. The ridges or little ridge may have been regarded as 'in front' of **Knockatoul**, 256728, 184 m., q.v. above.

Drummasor, 279726, Kirkcowan, 142 m.: possibly *druim màsbharra*, 'ridge of the buttock-shaped height'.

Drumshalloch, 282732, Kirkcowan, 180 m.; 312722, Penninghame, 102 m.; **Drumshalloch Loch**, 287737, Penninghame: Maxwell may be right in deriving-shalloch from *sealg*, 'hunting, fowling, fishing'. Possibly *druim seilg*, 'ridge where hunting, fowling or fishing take place', but *druim seileach*, 'willow ridge', is also possible.

Drumloskie, 305721, Penninghame, 122 m.: *druim losgaidh*, 'hill of burning', a beacon hill, or one where fire-ceremonies like Beltane were celebrated.

Drumadien, 275718, Kirkcowan, 135 m.: second element unclear; perhaps *dian*, on which Joyce (Joyce 1870, 296) comments: 'In the north of Ireland, the *ng* in the middle of the word *daingean* is pronounced as a soft guttural, which as it is very faint, and quite incapable of being represented by English letters, is suppressed in modern spelling, thereby changing *daingean* to *dian* or some such form'. A form *daigheann* for *daingeann* occurs in Scottish Gaelic. If this applies here, Drumadien is *druim daighinn*, 'fortress ridge', with an epenthetic vowel between the two elements of the name; compare also **East Dian**, 258707, 190 m.

Drummatrane, 261707, Kirkcowan, 135 m.: *druim na traighne*, 'ridge of the corncrake'.

Drumley, 251706, Kirkcowan, 202 m.: *druim liath*, 'grey ridge'. Maxwell suggests *druim laogh*, 'ridge of the calves' or 'of the young deer, fawns'.

Drummiemickie, 226703, Kirkcowan, 182 m.: *druim muice*, 'pig ridge', with intermediate epenthetic vowel.

Drumbain, 297689, Kirkcowan, 127 m.: *druim bàn*, 'white, lea ridge'.

Drumatier Plantation, 375683, Penninghame: *druim an t-saoir*, 'the carpenter's ridge', or 'McIntyre's ridge', with initial *mac* dropped as usual.

Drumstubbin, 258681, Kirkcowan, 177 m.: *druim stobain*, 'little stump ridge'.

Drumabrennan, 295670, Kirkcowan, habitation, 102 m.: *druim breunain*, 'dunghill ridge', with intermediate epenthetic vowel.

Drumalloch, 275666, Kirkcowan, habitation, 117 m.: *druim malaich*, 'ridge of the brow of the hill'.

Drumawa, 258657, Kirkcowan, 125 m.: possibly *druim a' bhath*, 'ridge of the snipe'.

Drumjin Wood, 381642, Penninghame: *druim dìona*, 'ridge of shelter'; cf. below, **Drumgin**. 406445, Glasserton.

Drumiemay, 286641, Kirkcowan, 115 m.: *druim a' m*[*h*]*aigh*, 'ridge of the plain', referring to the flat surface of **Drummurrie Moss**, 283637; *magh* sometimes refers to bog lands; cf. the situation of **The May**, 301514, Mochrum, habitation, and **Doon of May**, 296514, Mochrum, prehistoric fort.

Drummurrie, 290639, Kirkcowan, habitation, 97 m.: 'Murray's ridge'.

Drumterlie Hill, 387636, Penninghame, 67 m.; **Drumterlie**, 389633, habitation; **Drumterlie Cottage**, 391634, habitation: *druim* [*an*] *t-èarlaide*, 'ridge of expectation, trust', probably referring to 'the right sometimes sold by an outgoing to an incoming tenant to enter into possession of the arable land early in spring – the incomer doing the ploughing, sowing and planting, and subsequently claiming the resulting crop. It is in vogue only in places where Whitsunday is the removal term for farmers' (Dwelly, s.v. *èarlaid*).

Drumawan (stress on the second syllable), 299634, Kirkcowan, 143 m.: Maxwell, following Joyce 1870, 196, suggests *druim Shamhuinn*, 'ridge of the festival of Samhuinn', the 1st of November, All Hallows, but previously a pagan festival, marking the beginning of winter, a time when the barrier between the living and the dead was believed to be open.

Drumawantie Hill, 377634, Penninghame, 83 m.: perhaps *druim a' chinnntaighe*, 'the chieftain's ridge'. If so, the reference is probably to the

McKie holder of the Merton barony.

Drumgowan, 402617, Penninghame, 42 m.: *druim* [*a'*] *g*[*h*] *obhainn*, 'the blacksmith's ridge', probably because a forge was located there to take advantage of the stronger draught on the hill. Maxwell suggests *druim gamhainn*, 'ridge of the stirks' or 'of the yearling deer'.

Drumaskimming, 357610, Penninghame, 55 m.: 'McSkimming's ridge'. McSkimming is still a reasonably common Galloway name.

Drumdennal, 356609, Penninghame, 68 m.: perhaps *druim teiníl*, 'lime-kiln ridge' or *druim tionail*, 'ridge of the mustering, armed assembly'. The *-d-* in *-dennal* may reflect the fact that *druim* was originally a neuter noun, nasalizing the initial consonant of the word following.

Maxwell, s.v., notes that 'Immense drifts of cockle shells on various parts of the coast are the only local sources of lime in this part of Galloway, and were largely worked for making shell mortar and for manure'.

Drumwhirns, 397602, Penninghame, 77 m.: *druim a' chuirn*, 'ridge of the cairn', with added English *-s* plural.

Drummore Hill, 335595, Kirkcowan, 72 m.: *druim mór*, 'big ridge'. It is slightly lower than the nearby **Drumbeg Hill**, but longer and bulkier.

Drumanee, 316594, Kirkcowan, 60 m.: *druim an fheidh*, 'ridge of the deer'.

Drumbeg Hill, 336594, Kirkcowan, 73 m.: **Drumbeg**, 336588, habitation: *druim beag*, 'little ridge'.

Molland Hill, 386593, Wigtown, 81m.; **Little Molland**, 386599, 69 m.; Pont, *Drummmollyinhill*, habitation: *druim muilinn*, 'mill ridge'. The hills together form the ridge, but in modern usage *druim* has been dropped. Cf. **Drummullin Burn**, 453371-477364, Whithorn.

Drumfeatherin, 393589, Penninghame, 77 m.: *druim Phaidrín*, 'little Patrick's ridge'.

Drumagee, 305587, Kirkcowan, 87 m.: *druim na gaoithe*, 'ridge of the wind', 'windy ridge'. Also possible is 'MacGhie's ridge'; cf. Balmaghie House, 717632, Balmaghie parish, in the Stewartry. The MacGhies were the leading family of Clenafren. Clenafren (MacGhie) and Clenconnon (MacLennan) were prominent Galloway clans.

Drumlane Hill, 407585, Wigtown, 67 m.: *druim leathann*, 'broad ridge'. It is close to **Auchleand**, 413588, q.v., c. 3.

Drumwhirran, 302584, Kirkcowan, 95 m.: *druim* [*a'*] *choirein*, 'ridge of the little cauldron'.

Drumwhillan, 309584, Kirkcowan, 103 m.: *druim chuilinn*, 'holly ridge'.

Drummonie, 312581, Kirkcowan, 92 m.: *druim mhonaidh*, 'moor ridge'.

Drumcagerie, 298579, Kirkcowan, 80 m.: *druim cathag-dhearg*, 'chough ridge' (the *-g-* in *-cagerie* is hard).

Drumwhirn, 287544, Mochrum, 100 m.: *druim a' chùirn*, 'ridge of the cairn'.

Drumwalt, 308538, Mochrum, habitation, 75 m.; **Moor of Drumwalt**, 3054: second element obscure. Watson 1926, 180, suggests a derivation from Welsh *gwellt*, 'grass', presumably combined with the Welsh cognate of *druim*, *trum*: *trum wellt*, 'grass ridge'.

Drumcauchlie, 338529, Mochrum, 77 m.: *druim chochail*, 'hood ridge'. The basic meaning of *cochull* is 'hood'; it is a borrowing of Latin *cucullus*. From this various meanings have been derived – 'husk', 'ear of barley', 'discarded skin of a snake', 'corn-cockle', 'bag', 'scrotum', and 'bush of furze', any one of which might have been applied to the ridge.

Drumnescat Burn, 339509, Mochrum; **Drumnescat Loch**, 338497; **Flow of Drumnescat**, 3450; *RMS* iv, 2208, 19 March 1574; 2285, 20 July 1574, *Drumnescart*; Pont, *Drummnescart*: The early forms suggest *druim an ascairt*, 'ridge of the tow', i.e. 'ridge where flax for the manufacture of tow is grown'. The modern forms suggest *druim neasgaide*, 'boil, pustule ridge', i.e. 'ridge shaped like a boil or pustule'. In either case, the ridge is probably now **Loch Hill**, 341504, 84 m., named from Drumnescat Loch.

Flow is Scots for 'a wet peat bog'.

The Drumnescat site is ideal for growing flax and processing it into tow; see MacQueen 2002, 23-4.

Drumjargon Hill, 410505, Kirkinner, 65 m.: **Drumjargon**, 409505, habitation: *druim deargain*, 'kestrel, hawk, redstart ridge' or *druim deargainn*, 'flea ridge', or *druim dearcain*, 'acorn ridge'.

Drumblair, 281503, Mochrum, habitation, 90 m.; Pont, *Drumblair*;

Drumblair Moor, 2851: *druim blair*, 'ridge of the peat-bog', with reference to Drumblair Moor.

Drumneil, 352478, Mochrum, habitation, 73 m.: 'Neil's ridge'.

Drumlochin, 322463, Mochrum, 52 m.: perhaps *druim lochain* or *lochna*, 'sea-grass ridge'.

Drumdarroch, 325461, Mochrum, 62 m.: *druim darrach*, 'oak-tree ridge'.

Drumscallan Hill, 378455, Mochrum, 63 m.: *druim sgalain*, 'hut ridge', probably referring to shieling huts.

Drummoddie, **North**, 396458, Glasserton, habitation; **West**, 390452, habitation; **East**, 395452, habitation; **South**, 391448, habitation; *RMS* iii, 2944, 27 July 1543, *Drummaddy*; Pont, *Drum-maddy*, habitation: *druim madaidh*, 'dog, fox, or wolf, ridge'. Also possible is *druim mòid*, 'court ridge', a Gaelic equivalent of the fairly common Court Hill, usually indicating the site of a baron court.

Drummonachan, 395456, Glasserton, 62 m.: *druim nan monachan* or *monaidhean*, 'ridge of the moors'. Possibly *druim manachain*, 'groin ridge'.

Drumwhodya, 355455, Mochrum, 48 m.: doubtful; perhaps *druim choitchinn*, 'ridge of common grazing'.

Drumskeog, **High**, 343454, Mochrum, habitation, 55 m.; *RMS* iv, 1173, 16 May 1557, *Drumskeok*; Pont, *Drumskioch*; **Low**, 339446, habitation, 32 m.: *druim sgiathach*, 'sheltering, protecting ridge'.

Drumtroddan Hill, 366450, Mochrum, 73 m.; **Drumtroddan**, 363499, habitation; Pont, *Drumtroddan*: *druim trodàin*, 'ridge of the skirmish, quarrel'.

Drumdon, 381448, Glasserton, 62 m.: *druim donn*, 'brown ridge'.

Drumbreach, 397448, Glasserton, 65 m.: *druim bruaich*, 'bank-ridge'. Maxwell suggests the archaic Irish *druim bréach*, 'ridge of the wolves'.

Drumcapenoch, 388447, Glasserton, 64 m.: *druim ceapanach*, 'ridge of little stumps'.

Drumacrae, 445447, Whithorn, 45 m.: 'Macrae's ridge'.

Drumtowl, 391446, Glasserton, 62 m.: *druim tuathal*, 'thwart ridge', probably in relation to **Drumcapenoch** and **Drumbreach** above.

Drumgin Hill, 406445, Glasserton, 72 m.; **Drumgin**, 406444, habitation: *druim dìona*, 'ridge of shelter'.

Drumrae Hill, 405433, Glasserton, 89 m.; **Drumrae**, 404432, habitation; **Low Drumrae**, 402433, habitation: *druim reídh*, 'smooth ridge'.

Drumfad, 371432, Mochrum, habitation, 35 m.: **Drumfad Bridge**, 371434, over the **Monreith Burn**; **High Drumfad**, 374433, habitation: *druim fada*, 'long ridge'.

Drumbeg Hill, 403428, Glasserton, 71 m.: *druim beag*, 'little ridge'.

Drummaston Hill, 459409, Whithorn, 64 m.; **Drummaston**, 460408, habitation: looks like *druim fhaistinne*, 'ridge of the prophecy, omen'. If so the reference is obscure.

Drumagilloch, 414403, Glasserton, 86 m.: looks like *druim na gealaich*, 'ridge of the moon', but this is unconvincing. Perhaps *druim cuilceach*, 'reedy ridge'.

Drumatye, **Kirk of**, 398374, Glasserton, 144 m.: on the south end of **Fell of Carleton**, 397375, 132 m.: *druim an taighe*, 'ridge of the house'. Maxwell notes: 'On the summit of Carleton Fell, where there is no house, but a singular ridge of rock, formed like a steeply pitched roof of a house. It goes also by the modern name of the Pratie Pit from its resemblance to a ridge or "pit" of stored potatoes.' Presumably it was also regarded as resembling the roof of a church.

Drummullin Burn, 453371-477364, Whithorn: *druim muilinn*, 'mill ridge'. The burn powered the mill, which was probably the ancestor of **Bysbie Mill**, 476366, Whithorn; see Donnachie 1971, 203.

Drummoral, 461361, Whithorn, habitation, 67 m.: *druim mór-bhaile*, 'ridge of the big homestead', referring probably to the promontory fort, 461362, situated on the ridge. In *mór-bhaile*, the second element, *baile*, is used in its earlier unspecialized sense.

Also to be noted is the name of a ridge in Kirkcowan parish, **Drums of Carsebuie**, 3265. The word *druim* was borrowed into Galloway Scots with the meaning 'an area of ridged land intersected by marshy hollows' (*SND*).

Maxwell gives a number of names which I have not been able to identify: ***Drumadug***, ***Drumguhan***, ***Drumjargon*** (Penninghame); ***Drumacarie***,

Drumandon, ***Drumatwoodie***, ***Drumbuie***, ***Drumchalloch***, ***Drumjenning***, ***Drumliebuie***, ***Drummaconnel***, ***Drumwave*** (Kirkcowan); ***Drummanochan*** (Wigtown); ***Drumdonnies***, ***Drumwhat*** (Mochrum).

Drumchalloch, Kirkcowan, is now perhaps represented by **Challoch Hill**, 322493, 92 m., or by **Big Challoch Hill**, 329582, 97 m., and **Little Challoch Hill**, 330579, 72 m. **Challoch** represents Gaelic *teallach*, 'fire-place', in particular 'smith's forge', often situated on higher ground to obtain a good draught. It is a common element in place-names.

(g) Glen-, Gaelic *gleann*, 'glen, valley'

Usually a river or stream gives a glen its name. Glenluce, for example, is the glen of the Water of Luce and extends over the full course of both Main and Cross Waters of Luce. In the Moors and Machars neither Bladnoch, Cree, Tarf nor Malzie has a glen; the word is confined to the valleys of much smaller streams, which modern field drainage has sometimes caused to disappear. Nor does the name of the stream always feature in the name of the glen. Names in *gleann* are relatively infrequent and for the most part occur in the Moors.

Glenvernoch, 345752, Penninghame, habitation; Pont, *Glenbarranach* ; **Glenvernoch Fell**, 332740, 184 m.; **Glenvernoch Wood**, 3575: looks like *gleann fearnach*, 'alder glen'. The form in Pont suggests *gleann beàrnach*, 'notched, gapped glen'. The glen is that of the **Boughty Burn**, i.e., 'burn with a fork or bend', a figurative use of Scots *bochty*, 'the first fork of a tree from the ground' (*SND*). A relatively late name, perhaps originating from a notable bend in the stream at Glenvernoch. The original stream name may have been *Fearnach*, 'abounding in alder'.

Glenjory, 333621, Kirkcowan: *gleann deòraidh*, 'glen of the outlaw', or, more probably, 'glen of the keeper of a relic'; see MacQueen 2002, 67.

Glenhowl Hill, 324595, Kirkcowan, 67 m.; *RMS* iv, 2202, 12 March 1574, *Glenhouill*; Pont, *Glenhowil*: The hill is a long way from Glenhowl, 208592, Old Luce, habitation, possibly *gleann an ubhail*, 'glen of the apple-tree', possibly *gleann na h-ula*, 'glen of the rank grass'.

Glenturk, 422571, Wigtown, habitation; *RMS* ii, 2138, 5 February 1493, 2337, 27 January 1497; 2799, 25 August 1504; 3275, 1 December 1508, *Glenturk*; Pont, *Glentuirck*; **Glenturk Moor Croft**, 417573, habitation; **Moorhead of Glenturk**, 414569, habitation: probably *gleann nan torc*, 'glen of the hogs, boars'. The stream forming the glen is the **Broken Causeway Burn**, the upper reach of the **Borrowmoss Burn**, names which fairly obviously are of recent origin;*-turk* may represent the earlier name for the stream. Gaelic *torc* does not appear as a stream-name elsewhere in Scotland, but the cognate *twrch* is frequent in Wales. If *twrch* is in fact the origin, Glenturk is another example of a Welsh (British) place-name in the Moors and Machars.

Glenling, **High**, 318513, Mochrum, habitation; Pont, *Glenling*; **Laigh**, 324519, habitation; **Glenling Moss**, 3251; **Glenling Burn**: perhaps *gleann linne*, 'glen of the pool'. The second element is unlikely to be Old Norse *lyng*, 'heather'.

Glentriplock, **High**, 357465, Mochrum, habitation; **Low**, 358462, habitation; *RMS* iv, 1173, 16 May 1557, *Glentroupleg*; Pont, *Glentrybloc*: *gleann tri-bhileag*, 'clover glen' (literally 'glen of the triple leaflet'). Pont places it on the right bank of a tributary of a stream flowing into Luce Bay just north of **Killantrae**. Ainslie's map places it on a tributary of the **Port William Burn**. Field-drainage has obscured the present-day situation.

Gleann Moigh, 418387, Glasserton, habitation: *gleann maigh*, 'glen of the plain'. The spelling suggests that the name has been given only recently. It does not appear on Pont or Ainslie's map.

Despite the modern spelling, four names have a basis other than *gleann*.

Glenruther, 322731, Penninghame, habitation; *RMS* iii, 532, 7 January 1528, *Clonriddin*; 1137, 16 February 1532, *Clonridder*; Pont *Klonnidder*; **Glenruther Lodge**, 321723, habitation: perhaps *cluain ridir*, 'knight's meadow', with a possible reference to the Knight's Templar or to the Knights of the Order of St. John.

Glenhapple, 374313, Penninghame, habitation; *RMS* iii, 10 January 1542, *Clonquhapill*; Pont, *Glenchappell*; **Glenhapple Fell**, 351701, 138 m.; Pont puts ***Chappell***, now presumably represented by the remains of **St Ninian's Chapel**, 377707, in the immediate neighbourhood: *cluain na seipeil*, 'meadow of the chapel'.

Glenrazie, 368683, Penninghame, habitation; *RMS* iii, 2576, 10 January 1542, *Clonrassy*; Pont, *Klonrassy*: *cluain rasach*, 'shrubby meadow'.

Glenvogie, 357675, Penninghame, habitation; Pont *Klonvogy*: *cluain a' bhogaich*, 'meadow of the quagmire'.

The confusion of *cluain* with *gleann* probably took place when Gaelic was on the point of disappearance as a spoken language.

(h) Knock-, Gaelic *cnoc*, 'hill, knoll'

As first element in a name, *cnoc* is represented on the modern map by Knock-. For the most part the referent is a hill, but sometimes a habitation, usually in the immediate neighbourhood of a hill, usually with the same name, but occasionally not. Several examples have already been mentioned: **Knockville**, 363724, Penninghame, habitation, *cnoc a' bhile*, 'hill of the ancient, venerated tree'; **Knockcuddy**, 378597, Penninghame, 88m., *cnoc udaig*, 'woodcock hill'; **Knocknamad**, 364580, Wigtown, 59 m., *cnoc na mbád*, 'hill of the boats'; **Knockmononday**, 368568, Wigtown, 37 m., *cnoc mon na h-annaide*, 'hill of the hill-ground of the *annaid*'. As might be expected, such names occur more frequently in the Moors than in the Machars. It is in the Machars, however, that they have more often become habitation-names.

I have noted two instances of *cnoc* as second, but defining, element, with prefixed adjective:

Shennock Fell, 313652, Kirkcowan, 195 m.; **Shennock**, 317660, habitation: *sean chnoc*, 'old hill'.

Glasnick, **High**, 352625, Penninghame; **Low**, 343618, both habitation: *glas chnoc*, 'green hill'.

Knockyclegy, 304751, Kirkcowan, 139 m.: *cnoc a' c[h]laiginn*, 'hill of the skull', probably with reference to its shape.

Knockernan, 259736, Kirkcowan, 184 m.: *cnoc Ernáin*, 'Ernan's hill'. The most celebrated Ernán was the maternal uncle of Columba, one of the monks who accompanied the saint to Iona. His death is described in Book 1, Chapter 45, of Adamnan's *Life of Columba* (Anderson 1991, 82-3). The name, however, was not uncommon.

Knockatoul, 256728, Kirkcowan, 184 m.: *cnoc tuathal*, 'thwart hill', in relation to **Druminnarbel**, 255730, and **Drummakibben**, 263731, q.v. Maxwell's *cnoc an t-sabhail*, 'hill of the barn' is possible, but it would be unexpected to find a barn in so remote a place.

Knockdown, 237717, Kirkcowan, 202m.: *cnoc donn*, 'brown hill'. Maxwell's *cnoc dùin*, 'fort hill', is theoretically possible, but there is no trace of a fort on the hill.

Knockanicken, 268716, Kirkcowan, 152m.: possibly, as Maxwell suggests, *cnoc a' chnocain*, 'hill of the little hill, tumulus', but perhaps *cnoc na h-inghne*, 'the girl's hill', 'the daughter's hill'.

Knockytinnie, 317683, Kirkcowan, 107 m.: *cnoc na teine* or *cnoc teineadh*, 'fire hill', perhaps indicating that it was a beacon hill or that it was the site for fire-festivals, such as Beltane on 1 May.

Knockhammy, 316672, Kirkcowan, 100 m.: *cnoc a' chamtha*, 'hill of the curve, crook'. A notable curve in the course of the **Black Burn** begins at the foot of this hill.

Knockstocks, 397668, Penninghame, habitation: *cnoc* [*nan*] *stoc*, 'hill of the (tree-)stumps', with English plural *-s* added.

Knockbrake, 276648, Kirkcowan, 130 m.; **Knockbrex, West**, 390645, habitation; **East**, 396642, habitation (*RMS* ii, 3018, 23 December 1506, *Knokbrakis*; Pont, *Knockbreck*); *Knockbrex Moor*, 397634, all Penninghame; **Knockbreck**, 287613, 107 m.; **Knockbreck**, 327606, 70 m., both Kirkcowan: *cnoc breac*, 'speckled hill'. In West and East Knockbrex English plural *-s* has been added, perhaps because the farm was divided at an early date.

Knockincar, 293646, Kirkcowan, 112 m.; **Knocknacor**, 351573, 52m.; **Knockencurr**, 425496, Kirkinner, habitation; **Knockencurr Cottage**, 433496, habitation: *cnoc an chuirre*, genitive of *corr*, which has a variety of meanings, 'projection', 'snout', 'angle', 'nook', 'corner', 'pit', 'hut', 'enclosure', 'pen', 'paddock', 'conical hill'.

Knockamuddy Wood, 390643, Penninghame, habitation: second element obscure.

Knockalanny, 277642, Kirkcowan, 140 m.: second element obscure.

Knock Henries, 257631, Kirkcowan, 92 m.: *cnoc éanarí*, 'hill of the fowlers', with English plural -*s* added. Maxwell follows Joyce 1871, 12, in suggesting *cnoc fhainre*, 'sloping hill'. The adjective *fainre* is not in the dictionaries, but is derived by Joyce from *fán*, 'slope'. Knock Henries is a series of gentle slopes on the left bank of the Tarf; 'hill of the slopes' would be an acceptable meaning.

Knock Roger, 265631, Kirkcowan, 112 m.: the second element is perhaps the personal name Roger. In consequence of his marriage to Helen, daughter of Alan, last Lord of Galloway (d. 1234), Roger de Quincy, 2nd Earl of Winchester (d. 1264), inherited, among much else, the barony of **Craighlaw**, 306611, Kirkcowan, which included Knock Roger, possibly a favourite spot for hunting or fishing.

Maxwell suggests *cnoc crochaire*, 'hangman's hill'. The hill, however, is remote from any likely court or prison site.

Knocklyoch, 279620, Kirkcowan, 103 m.: apparently *cnoc leitheach*, 'half-way hill'. Possibly *cnoc cleitheach*, 'secret hill'. In either case the reference is obscure.

Knockravie, 323612, Kirkcowan, 79 m.: *cnoc craobhach*, 'wooded hill'.

Knockskeog, 390587, Wigtown, 77 m.; **Knockskeog Farm**, 390584, habitation: *cnoc sgitheig*, 'hawthorn-tree hill'.

Knockronie, 385582, Wigtown, 79 m.: *cnoc cruinne*, 'hill of roundness', referring to its shape.

Knockcocher, 354580, Kirkcowan, 48 m.: *cnoc uachdair*, Old Irish *cnocc òchtair*, 'hill of the upper part', i.e., the South. The hill stands above a locally important crossroad, not far from **Spittal Bridge** over the Bladnoch, and marked the crossing place from the northern part of the early, undivided, Kirkinner parish, now Kirkcowan parish, to the southern, the modern Kirkinner parish; cf. in Ireland, for instance, the provincial names *Uachtar Connacht*, 'South Connaught' and *Íochtar Connacht*, 'North Connaught'. So too *Uachtar* and *Íochtar Urmhumhan*, the baronies of Upper and Lower Ormond in Co. Tipperary. Kirkcowan was still a pendicle of Kirkinner in 1435 (Cowan 1967,).

Knockmore Hill, 390572, Wigtown, 62 m.; **Knockmore**, 390573, habitation: *cnoc mór*, 'big hill'.

Knockann, 419511, Kirkinner, habitation; Pont *Knokkan*: *cnoc abhann*, 'hill of the stream', with reference to the **Kirkland Burn**, which flows past Knockann and onwards through **Kirkinner**. Nowadays land drainage has reduced the burn to a ditch, but on Pont's map it seems a more prominent feature.

Knockeffrick Hill, 419442, Kirkinner, 91 m.; **Knockeffrick**, 419491, habitation: the second element is probably *Affrica*, the name of the daughter of Fergus, 1st Lord of Galloway (d. 1161). She married Ólafr Goddredsson I, king of Mann (d. 1153). Fergus's chief stronghold at **Cruggleton** is at no great distance.

Knocknishie, 447554, Whithorn, 47 m.: *cnoc nise*, 'weasel hill'.

Knocknar, 342430, Mochrum, 39 m.: *cnoc an àir*, 'hill of the ploughing', possibly *cnoc an aoghaire*, 'hill of the herdsman'. Dwelly notes, s.v., 'The *aoighairean* of the Hebrides, according to Pennant, are farm servants who have the charge of cultivating a certain portion of land and of overseeing the cattle it supports. They have grass for 2 milch cows and 6 sheep, and also one tenth sheaf of the produce of the said ground, and as many potatoes as they chose to plant.'

Knock, 370410, Glasserton, habitation (*RMS* iv, 2823, *Knok de Kirkmadin*; Pont, *Knock*); **Low Knock**, 374403, habitation; **Knock Wood**, 370405: *cnoc*, 'hill'. Knock stands at an 85 m. altitude.

Knockgulsha, 385381, Glasserton, 60 m.: Maxwell suggests the Irish Gaelic *cnoc giolcaighe*, 'hill of reeds', Scots Gaelic *cnoc cuilceich*, 'hill of the reedy fen'. This does not particularly fit the local topography; Knockgulsha is at the top of a cliff, topped by a steep coastal slope, above Luce Bay. Moreover, the *-c-* in *giolcaighe* would not give rise to *-sh-*. Phonetically, *cnoc goillseach*, 'distressing hill' fits better. Distress would certainly result from any attempt to carry herring from **Lochanscadden**, 379381, on the shore below to Knockgulsha. Cf. Knockgilsie, NW 991714, Kirkcolm, 84 m., also a steep slope, and perhaps the lost ***Auchengilshie***, Kirkinner.

Knockanharrie, 474359, Whithorn, 35 m.: Maxwell suggests *cnocan fhaire*, 'watch hillock' (*cnocan*, diminutive of *cnoc*). The similarity of Knockenharry Hill, NW 982674, Kircolm, suggests *cnoc na h-àirighe*, 'hill of the shieling'.

Maxwell lists several names which I have not been able to identify: ***Knockmulloch***, ***Knockroid***, Kirkcowan, ***Knockaldie***, ***Knockietowl***, Penninghame, ***Knockcroe***, ***Knockdon***, ***Knockentarry***, Mochrum.

(i) Suffixed *–ach*, *-och*, *-ie*

These suffixes are fairly common in Gaelic place-names and have two main origins. Sometimes they represent original *–ach* (for earlier *-acum-*), an adjectival suffix denoting possession 'or – when added to words descriptive of place – residence or situation in the place in question' (Thurneysen 1946, 220). The root word to which the suffix is attached is usually recognisable. Where *-ie* is found, it represents the dative-locative form of *-ach, -aidh*.

Such names are likely to be early – i.e., well before 1000 AD. The form has a long history in the Celtic languages. Names of French towns and villages ending in *-ac* or *-y*, – Pauillac, Champagnac, Fleury are familiar examples – in Gallo-Roman times were the estates of Paulus, Campanius and Florius respectively, formed by adding *-acum* to the names of the owners.

The semantic effect is sometimes minimal. Joyce remarks (Joyce 1872, 5): 'the termination *ach* is often added to a word for no apparent reason except to form "a sort of finish", without in any way changing the meaning of the word'.

In some instances, however, *-ach* is not a suffix, but represents the defining, unstressed second element of a compound. Cf. Challoch, discussed in chapter 6 (c) below.

Fyntalloch (now the name of a small loch adjacent to Loch Ochiltree), 314740, Penninghame, Pont *O*[*vir*]. *Fintilloch*, *N*[*ethir*]. *Fintillochs*, habitations (on Pont's map the loch does not appear; it apparently was continuous with Loch Ochiltree): *fionnt*(*h*)*ulach*, 'white, fair hillock'; *tulach* from *tul*, 'prominence, eminence, hillock'.

Jultock Point, 489490, Sorbie (on Wigtown Bay): *ealtach* (from *ealt*, 'covey, drove, flock'), 'place of flocks of birds', 'place abounding in birds'.

Corhulloch, 340468, Mochrum, habitation; Pont, *Karhallach*; **Corhulloch Hill**, 339469, 103 m.; *RMS* iv, 2208, 19 March 1574, *Corhalluchhill*; **Corhulloch Cottage**, 339466, habitation: *corrthulach*, 'odd, out-of-the-way hillock'.

Falclintalloch, Mochrum: *fàl cluaine tulaich*, 'turf-dyke of hillock-meadow', or *fàl glin tulaich*, 'turf-dyke of hillock-glen'. See below, chapter 6 (f) . The name is listed by Maxwell, but I have not been able to locate it on the modern map.

Mulloch, 302723, Penninghame, 147 m.; **Lump of the Mulloch**, 298695, Kirkcowan, habitation; **Mulloch Park**, 295693; **Mulloch**, 375628, Penninghame, habitation; **Mulloch Hill**, 377628, 86 m.: *mullach*, 'top, summit (-place)', from *mul* or *mol*, 'top, summit'.

In Scots *lump* sometimes means 'piece, portion of land'. *SND* quotes from the first *Statistical Account* of Scotland (1795): 'Land is not let by the acre, but by the piece or *lump*'. **Mulloch Park** is probably the original *Lump*, **Lump of the Mulloch** the farm-name.

Beoch, 321718, Penninghame, habitation; *RMS* iii, 532, 7 January 1528, 1137, 16 February 1532, *Beauch*; Pont, *Byochs*; **Beoch Bridge**, 313714, over **Beoch Burn**, flowing from Loch Ochiltree into the Bladnoch: *beitheach*, 'place of birches, birch wood' (from *beith*, 'birch tree'). The form in Pont has English plural -*s* added.

Blairoch, 313711, Penninghame: probably from *blàr*, which sometimes means 'a bare exposed place as distinguished from a sheltered site' (Dinneen); *blàrach* (a hypothetical form), 'bare, exposed place'.

Glassoch, 337696, Penninghame, habitation; *RMS* ii, 1624, 16 August 1485, *Glassauchfurde* (across the **Bladnoch**); 3018, 23 December 1506, *Glassacht*; 3134, 6 September 1507, *Glasachy* (for *Glasacht*?); Pont, *Glassoch*, *Glassoch Lochs*; **Glassoch Fell**, 337709, 152 m.; **Glassoch Wood**, 338699; **Glassoch Bridge** (across the Bladnoch, replacing *Glassauchfurde*), 333696: *glaiseach*, 'place of streams, watery bogland', from *glais*, 'stream', now obsolete in Scottish Gaelic.

At present, two burns flow into the Bladnoch at Glassoch. The lochs on Pont's map have been drained.

Ballochadee, 296653, Kirkcowan, habitation*: bealach àth d*(*h*) *uibh*, 'black ford pass'. The ford is across the **Ballochadee Burn**, which, a mile or so farther on, flows into the **Black Burn**. A track runs through Ballochadee to **Barnharrow**.

Bealach probably from early Irish *bil*, 'mouth'.

Ballochrae Wood, 315611, **Hill**, 317606, 69 m., and **Burn**, Kirkcowan: *bealach réidh*, 'smooth, level pass'. A by-road and the line of the old railway go through the likely site of this pass.

Maxwell also gives ***Ballochmyre***, Penninghame, and ***Ballochmagour***, Whithorn, neither of which I have been able to identify.

Lurneoch, 362626, Penninghame, habitation: *luachairneach*, 'place where rushes grow', from *luachair*, 'rush'. Lurneoch is on the edge of **Merton Hall Moss**, 3662, Penninghame.

Tintock Hill, 367517, Mochrum, 98 m.: *teinteach*, 'place of fire' (from *teine*, 'fire'), originally, perhaps, a beacon-hill or a place for Beltane fire-celebrations.

Capenoch, 380508, Kirkinner, habitation; **Capenoch Croft**, 382515, habitation: *ceapanach*, 'place of tree-stumps' from *ceap*, 'block'.

Larroch, 372408, Glasserton, habitation; *RMS* iii, 2944, 27 July 1543, Laroch; **Larroch Cottage**, 376407: *làrach*, with various meanings, 'site', 'ruin', 'habitation', 'abode', farm', from *làr*, which has two basic meanings, 'surface' and 'middle'; the most common derivative sense is 'floor'. Larroch most probably means simply 'farm', perhaps 'old farm'.

Enoch, 443393, Whithorn, habitation: *aonach*, 'meeting-place', 'fair', 'moor'; from *aon*, 'one (the numeral)'. Alternatively *eanach*, 'marsh', from *èan*, 'water'. On the southern outskirts of the burgh of Whithorn.

Craigie, 341736, Penninghame, habitation: dative/locative of *creagach*, 'rocky (place)', from *creag*, 'rock, cliff'; 'at rocky place'.

Tannylaggie, 287720, Kirkcowan, habitation; Pont *O*[*vir*]. *Tynalaggach*, *Nether Tyna-laggach*; **Tannylaggie Bridge** (over the **Bladnoch**), 291720: dative/locative of the feminine form of *tamhnach*, 'clearing' (possibly from *tamhan*, 'tree-stump'), apparently combined with the adjective *lagach*, one meaning of which is 'full of dens, pits or hollows'; 'at clearing filled with dens, pits or hollows'. The word *tamhnach* seems to exist only in place-names, for the most part in the north and west of Ireland. It is fairly wide-spread in SW Scotland, but does not seem to occur in the north. Maxwell has ***Tannoch*** in Penninghame parish which I have not been able to identify.

Tannyflux, 312675, Kirkcowan, habitation: *tamhnaigh fliuch*, 'at wet clearing', with English plural *-s* added.

Cairny Hill, 286702, Kirkcowan, 162 m.: dative/locative, *càrnaigh*, of *càrnach*, 'cairn-place, stony place', from *càrn*, 'cairn': 'at cairn-place'.

Clauchrie, 409563, Wigtown, habitation; Pont *Clachary*; **Clauchrie Moor**, 4056; **Clauchrie**, 406532, Kirkinner, habitation; Pont, *Clachory*: dative/locative of *clochrach*, 'stony place', from *cloch*, 'a stone'; 'at stony place'. In Pont an epenthetic vowel is inserted between *-ch-* and *-r-*, a normal feature of spoken Gaelic.

Smirie Wood, 434357, Glasserton: *smeuraigh*, dative/locative of *smeurach*: 'at place of brambles (*smeur*)'.

The following names are in fact compounds:

Brockloch Hill, 221721, Kirkcowan, 212 m.; **Brocklock**, 252637, Penninghame: *broclach*, 'badger set, den', from *broc*, 'badger' and *luch*, *loch*, 'hole'; cf. **Challoch** below, chapter 6.

Crailloch, 324524, Mochrum, habitation; *RMS* iv, 1436, 16 December 1562, *Craluch*; Pont, *Krellach*; **Crailloch Mote**, 325526: etymology obscure. Maxwell suggests *criothlach*, 'shaking bog', which gives rise to such Irish place-names as Creelogh and Creelagh.. There is bog land nearby, but phonetically Crailloch seems unlikely as a reflex of *criothlach*. The first element is possibly not *crith*, but the cognate *crath*, both meaning 'act of shaking': the literal meaning of the hypothetical *crathluch* would be 'shaking loch' or 'shaking hollow'. Compare *crathrach*, 'shaking bog'.

Boyach, 472365, Whithorn, habitation; Pont, *Buyesh*; **Boyach Loch**, 466360: perhaps *bó-theach*, 'cow-house, byre', from *bó*, 'cow' and *teach*, 'house'.

Morrach, 467350, Whithorn, habitation; Pont, *Moroch*: *mormhoich*, dative/locative, 'at sea-plain', 'at the level ground by the sea', from *mor*, compositional form of *muir*, 'sea', and *magh*, 'level ground, plain'.

Chapter 6

More Gaelic Name-Elements

(a) Blair-, *blàr*, 'field, battle, peat-moss'; May, *magh*, 'plain, field'; Inch-, *innis*, 'island, meadow'; Carse-, 'the stretch of low alluvial land along the banks of some Scottish rivers'

These words indicate the flatness, usually also the wetness, of the land so named. 'Moss' or 'bog' would often be an appropriate translation. The first three are Gaelic, usually appearing on modern documents as Blair, May and Inch. *Carse* is not Gaelic, but in the Moors and Machars, as in Galloway generally, is used as if it were, forming so-called 'inversion-compounds', where the structure is Gaelic – i.e., the defining element comes first, the stressed qualifier second – but the defining element is Germanic, usually Norse. One example, **Carseriggan**, 316677, Kirkcowan, habitation, has already been mentioned in chapter 1, as have the similarly constructed *Kirk-* names in chapter 4. See too Ekwall 1918, and MacQueen 1956. Inversion compounds mark the presence of the *Gall-Ghaidhil.*

For all four words the usual reference is to flat bog-land, used both for pasture and for the cutting of peat. Bog-land is almost as characteristic of the Moors and Machars as it is of midland Ireland. The fairly frequent **Auchness**, *each innis*, 'horse meadow', shows that, at least sometimes, the pasture was for horses, probably the once well-known 'Galloway naigs'.

Blairgower, 297722, Penninghame: *blàr gobhar*, 'goat-moss'.

Blairmoddie, 288718, Kirkcowan, habitation: *blàr madaidh*, 'moss of the dog/wolf/fox'.

Blair Hill, 274724, Kirkcowan, 147 m.: 'hill above Blood Moss'

Blairderry, 268620, Kirkcowan, habitation; *RMS* iv, 2202, 12 March 1574, *Blairdirry*: *blàr doire*, 'oak-tree moss'. See below, (c), *doire.*

Blairnagobber, 281617, Kirkcowan: *blàr na gabair*, 'moss of the goat'; *gabar* is a variant form of *gobhar.*

Blair Hill, 377549, Kirkinner, 29 m.: 'hill above the moss, the marshy land along the Bladnoch'.

Blairmakin Muir, 412509, Kirkinner, habitation; Pont, *Blairmakin*: perhaps the name is a hybrid, 'moss of the malt-kiln'. The **Maltkiln Burn** flows nearby.

Blairshinnoch, 368467, Kirkinner, habitation; *RMS* iii, 1516, 30 September 1535, *Blairschynnauch*; **Blairshinnoch Bridge** (over **Killantrae Burn**), 365466; **Blairshinnoch Hill**, 369469, 66 m.: *blàr sionnach*, 'fox moss'. The moss is the land between the Killantrae Burn and the **Barmullan Burn**.

High Blair, 434472, Sorbie, habitation; **Low Blair**, 438471, habitation; *RMS* ii, 2056, 9 September 1491, *Blayr*; 2975, 17 July 1506, *Blare*; **Blair Hill**, 432472, 65 m. The reference is to the great moss at Sorbie.

Blairbuy, 362419, Glasserton, habitation; *RMS* ii, 3394, 24 December 1509, *Blareboy*; **Blairbuy Loch**, 364417; **Blairbuie Bridge** (over **Monreith Burn**), 358418: *blàr buidhe*, 'yellow moss'.

Compare too above, chapter 5, **Drumblair**, 281503, Mochrum.

The May, 301514, Mochrum, habitation; Pont, *May*; **Doon of May**, 296514, prehistoric fort: *magh*, 'plain, moss', referring to the surrounding bog-lands. **Doon** is *dun*, 'fort'.

Cf. above, chapter 5, **Drumiemay**, 286641, Kirkcowan.

Inshanks,, Kirkcowan; Pont, *Inchacks*: *innis eanga*, 'angle-moss'.

Auchness Hill, 356585, Wigtown, 42m. (on the left bank of the Bladnoch): *each innis*, horse meadow. The first element, **Auch-**, takes the stress, thus demonstrating that it is not *achadh*, 'field'.

Auchness Hill, 337583, Kirkcowan, 52 m.(on bog-land beside the **Clugston Burn**); **Auchness Wood**, 3458: *each innis*.

Inchmulloch Hill, 282571, Kirkcowan, 100 m.: *innis mullaich*, 'moss of the top, height'. The hill is surrounded by bog-land.

Claunch, 427481, Sorbie, habitation; Pont, *Cloyinsh*; **Claunch Cottages**, 427478: *cladh-innis*, 'ditch-meadow'.

Inch, 447474, Sorbie, habitation; Pont, *Ynch*: *innis*, 'moss, meadow'. The farm is in the midst of the moss at Sorbie.

Auchness, 399433, Glasserton, habitation; *Auchness Moss*, 3943: *each innis*, 'horse meadow'. Situated in the bog-land surrounding **White Loch**, 400440.

Carsindarroch Knowes, 301707, Kirkcowan; **Carsindarroch Steps** (a series of waterfalls on the Bladnoch), 313707: *carse nan darach*, 'carse of the oak-trees'.

Carseriggan, 316677, Kirkcowan, habitation; **Carseriggan Crag**, 313608, 115 m.; **Carseriggan Moor**, 3169: see above, chapter 1.

Carsenestock, 445620, Penninghame, habitation; Pont, *Carsnestak*: second element obscure.

Carsegowan, 420586, Wigtown, habitation; Pont *Carsgawin*; **Carsegowan Moss**, 4258: probably 'Gavin's (portion of the) carse'. Alternatively, *carse gobhain*, 'the smith's (portion of the) carse'.

Carselae, 433583, Wigtown, habitation: *carse laogh*, 'calf-meadow'. In this and the previous two examples, the carse is that of the Cree and its tributary, the Bishop Burn.

Carseduchan, **High**, 368480, Mochrum, habitation; **Low**, 363472, habitation; Pont, *Karsducchan*: perhaps *carse duthcha*, 'carse of the district', indicating a common pasture. The carse appears to be that of the Killantrae Burn and an unnamed tributary.

(b) Derry, Dar-, Der-, Dir-, Old Irish *daire*, *doire*, 'oak wood', 'thicket'

In recent times the Forestry Commission has planted woods over much former bog land. In a way, they have repeated a process which began more spontaneously in the aftermath of the last Ice Age. 'By c. 5500 BC Galloway was covered in forest consisting chiefly of oak, elm and hazel, together with alder, ash and a range of smaller trees and shrubs' (Murray 2006, 8). The trees themselves contributed to the growth of peat-bogs, which in turn provided an effective seeding-ground for more trees, which were still numerous in the earliest historic period. Most were subsequently felled, but place-names provide evidence for their existence. The basic meaning of Old Irish *daire*, *doire*, is 'a wood of oak trees', from which develops the more generalised meaning 'grove, thicket', not necessarily of oaks. In modern names the word in isolation occurs as 'Derry', in the first element of compounds as 'Dar-', 'Der-' or 'Dir-'.

Bog-oak, 'the wood of oak preserved in a black state in peat-bogs etc.' (*OED*), provides the clearest evidence for these ancient trees. See, for example, Samuel Robinson's description of the parish school at Barglass, Kirkinner, in the closing years of the eighteenth century (Robinson 1872, 19): 'There were three writing desks with benches to suit, of foreign timber, at one end of the room; the seats for the other classes were of a very homely character. They were old oak trees which had been dug out of the mosses of the neighbourhood, nearly as when they were found, as far as polishing was concerned, and propped up to suit the length of the lower limbs of his majesty's young subjects, the props being rough blocks of stone, or earthen sods.'

High Derry, 268747, Kirkcowan, habitation: *daire*.

Darloskine, 2774, Kirkcowan; **Darloskine Bridge** (over the Bladnoch), 279729: *daire losgann*, 'toad thicket, thicket where toads abound'.

Derry, 260734, Kirkcowan, habitation: *daire*.

Dargodjel, 297727, Penninghame: second element obscure.

Dernakissoch, 261715, Kirkcowan: probably *doire an cheasaich*, 'thicket of the road over boggy ground'.

Dirvananie, 229703, Kirkcowan, habitation; Pont, *Dyrrymannany*: second element obscure. It may be the possessive *mo*, 'my', followed by the name of some saint, just possibly Ninian under the original form of the name, *Nyniau*. Maxwell suggests *doire Mhananaich*, 'Manxman's oak-grove', which presupposes a wrong stress-pattern.

Dirneark, 261703, Kirkcowan, habitation; *RMS* iv, 1663, 26 August 1565, *Dalniark*; Pont, *Dyrnairp*; **Gall Moss of Dirneark**, 2668: *doire na h-earc*, 'thicket of the heifer' or 'of the pig'. *Gall* is the shrub *Myrica gale*, sweet gale or bog-myrtle.

The name obviously gave some trouble. In *RMS* the more familiar *Dal-* has been substituted, probably for *Dar-*. Pont recognised the first element, but misheard or miscopied the second.

Dargoal, **Burn**, 2771, Kirkcowan; **Hill**, 282695; *RMS* ii, 2521, 14 February 1500, *Derregill*, habitation; iv, 2202, 12 March 1574, *Dirgollis*, habitation; Pont, *Dyrgaals*, habitation: *daire gobhal*, 'oakgrove of the forks, forked trees'. Forked timbers were used in the roofs of crucked buildings. In the second *RMS* form and in Pont, English plural *-s* has been added.

Dirvachlie, 249701, Kirkcowan, habitation; *RMS* iv, 1663, 6 August 1565, *Dalvauchlyne (sive Darvauchlyne)*; Pont, *Dyrvachly*: *doire bhachlae*, 'grove of the crozier'. Reference obscure. For the second element Maxwell suggests *buachaille*, 'of the cow-herd' or, less probably, 'of the shepherd'. For the forms in *RMS*, cf. **Dirneark** above.

Dirnow, 290654, Kirkcowan, habitation; **Dirnow Hill**, 291656, 107 m.: *doire naomh*, 'holy wood'. Again, the reference is obscure.

Derrie, 329500, Mochrum, habitation; *RMS* iv, 2208, 19 March 1574, *Dirre*; Pont, *Dyrry*; **Derry Hill**, 333509, 107 m.; **Flow of Derrie**, 3349: *doire*.

Dernafranie Hill, 289571, Mochrum, 107 m.: looks like *doire na fraigh-shnighe*, 'thicket of the water flowing through a boundary, partition'. The hill is close to the boundary between Mochrum and Kirkinner parishes. A tributary of the **Drumdow Burn** flows across the boundary directly under the hill.

Flow of Darsnag, 3254, Mochrum: *daire snag*, 'woodpecker thicket'. The Gaelic for the great spotted woodpecker is *snagan-daraich*, literally 'little woodpecker of the oak tree'. *Daire*/*doire* and *darach* are both derived from the same root. Cf. also **Kildarroch**, above, chapter 4(b).

In Galloway-Scots, *Flow* means 'a wet peat-bog, a morass'.

Maxwell consistently interprets Dar-, Der-, Dir- as *dur*, earlier *dobhar*, 'water, stream'. This is improbable. *Dur*/*dobhar* is an archaic word, which survives either in isolation, as in *Dover* or the French river-name *Douvres*, or as the second element in a compound place-name, Aber*dour*, for instance, or the river-name Cal*der*. The origin is usually Welsh (British) or Gaulish rather than Gaelic. I have found no single instance of the word as first element in a compound place-name, much less of such a cluster as Maxwell proposes.

(c) Challoch-, *teallach*, 'blacksmith's forge'

Old Irish *tellach*, earlier *tenlach*, is formed from *teine*, 'fire' and *luch*, *loch*, which usually means 'lake', but also 'hollow, hole'; cf. the cognate Greek λάκκος, 'pit'. There may also be some confusion with Old Irish *loc*, 'place', probably a borrowing from Latin *locus*, 'place'. In later Irish and Scottish Gaelic *tellach* becomes *teallach*, with slender *t*-, pronounced almost like *ch*- in 'cheerful'. The primary meaning is 'hole for a fire, fireplace, hearth'; eventually it acquired the specialised meaning 'blacksmith's forge'. It is in this sense that the word occurs in Scottish, not Irish, place-names; the usual English transliteration is 'Challoch'. To obtain the maximum draught from the wind, forges were usually placed on or near the summit of a hill. The forges have long since disappeared, but the name Challoch survives, sometimes as a habitation name.

Challock Cairn, 372684, Penninghame, 57m.

Challoch, 385669, Penninghame, habitation; *RMS* iii, 2576, 10 January 1542, *Challoch*; Pont *Chellach*; **Challoch Hill**, 384669, 47 m.; **Challoch Moss**, 382665; **Challoch Burn**.

Challochglass, 297549, Mochrum, habitation; *RMS* iv, 2208, 19 March 1574, *Challuchglas*; 2285, 20 July 1574, *Challachglas*; Pont *Shellachglash*; **Challochglass Moor**, 2855; **Challochglass Moss**, 2955: *teallach glas*, 'green forge'. It stands on a stony ridge (114 m.) above the green expanse of the surrounding bog-land.

Big Challoch Hill, 328582, Kirkcowan, 67 m.; **Little Challoch Hill**, 330579, 72 m.

Fell of Craighalloch, 333546, Mochrum, 118 m.; **Craighalloch Moor**, 3354; Pont, *Keryhalloch*: ? *ceathramh an teallaich*, 'quarter-land of the forge'.

Challoch Hill, 321494, Mochrum, 92 m.

Challoch Hill, 439417, Whithorn, 83 m.

North Challochblewn Plantation, 418385, Glasserton; **South**, 413376; Pont *Chellachblawis*: second element obscure. It may be the Wigtownshire surname Blain, short for MacBlain, a name commemorating Bláán, a late 6th-century saint, bishop of Kingarth in

Bute and patron of Dunblane Cathedral.

(d) Eldrig, *eileirg*, 'deer-trap'

The rare Old Irish word *erelc* means 'an ambush'. In Scottish Gaelic both meaning and form were changed. The word underwent metathesis, becoming *eileirg* or *eileirig*, and, perhaps by association with *èilid*, 'hind, female of the red deer, roe', acquired the specialised meaning 'deer-trap'. Watson (Watson 1926, 489) comments: 'The *eileirg* was a defile, natural or artificial, wider at one end than at the other, into which the deer were driven, often in hundreds, and slain as they passed through. The slaughter at the *eileirg* was the last stage in the great deer hunts which were once so common in Scotland and which survived in the north till the eighteenth century.'

This kind of hunt was found in England as well as Scotland; cf., e.g., the hunt in the fourteenth-century poetic romance, *Sir Gawain and the Green Knight*, 1146-73. It should be noted that the hinds, rather than the male deer, were the target of this kind of hunt. One of the duties of the beaters was to separate the harts from the hinds.

In place-names, *eileirg* usually becomes Eldrig, Elrig or Elrick. It is sometimes possible to identify the defile which gave rise to the name.

Rather surprisingly, where *eileirg* has survived, it is usually as a habitation name. From this it has sometimes been applied to other natural features.

White Eldrig, 248753, Kirkcowan, habitation.

Fell of Eldrig of Liberland, 247746, Kirkcowan. For **Liberland** see below chapter 8 (b).

Eldrig, High, 250691, Kirkcowan, habitation; **Low**, 251679, habitation; **Eldrig Moss**, 2569; **Eldrig Loch**, 253614; **Eldrig Fell**, 252686, 227 m.

Eldrig, Meikle, 349674, Penninghame, habitation; *RMS* ii, 3018, 23 December 1506, *Meikle Elrik*; 3134, 16 September 1507, *Heilrikmore*; **Little**, 345661, habitation; *RMS*, *ut supra*, *Litil Elrik*, *Neilrigbeg*. The Gaelic qualifiers in the two slightly later entries, *mór*, big', and *beag*, ‘little’, probably indicate that in the early years of the sixteenth century Gaelic as well as Scots was still spoken in the area.

Elrig, 321474, Mochrum, habitation; *RMS* iii, 1912, 10 February 1539, *Alrig*; iv, 2208, 19 March 1574, *Elrig*; **Elrig Loch**, 3249; **Elrig Fell**, 331485, 132 m.; **Elrig Farm**, 327481.

(e) Pal-, Pol-, Pul-: Gaelic *poll*; Alt-: Scots Gaelic *allt*, ‘a stream, burn’

W.J. Watson (Watson 1926, 204) noted that the use of *poll*, usually ‘pool, a hole, mud’, in the sense of a slow stream is common in SW Scotland. An instance from outside our immediate area is Polmadie in Glasgow, so called from the Polmadie Burn which flows into the Clyde at Polmadie Bridge. Watson regarded this feature as ‘rather Welsh than Gaelic’, i.e., as an adaptation and extension to Gaelic of names once containing the cognate Welsh *pwll*, ‘pool, puddle, pit’. Such names are commoner in Wales than names in *poll* in other parts of Scotland and in Ireland; the *Melville Richards Place-Name Archive* (*MRPNA*) in the University of Wales, Bangor, lists no less than 4232, with Pwllheli, SH3735, Caernarvon, ‘pool of salt water’, perhaps the most familiar. In all examples, however, *pwll* appears to mean ‘pool’, ‘hole’ or ‘pit’; so far as I know, there is no instance of ‘slow-moving stream’. Names like Aberpwll, ‘confluence of the pool’, might conceivably give rise to the idea that at least sometimes it might become the name of a stream, but there is no certain instance.

The etymology of *poll* and *pwll* is uncertain. They may be borrowings from Anglo-Saxon *pol* (with long -*o*-), ‘pool’, ‘deep place in a river’, ‘tidal stream’. But the use of *pwll* in Welsh place-names is so widespread that this seems unlikely.

A possible alternative is Latin *palus*, genitive *paludis*, ‘marsh, bog’. By metathesis there emerged from the stem *palud*- a late form **padul*-, preserved, for instance in Italian *padule*, Spanish *paúl*, Portuguese *paul*, ‘marsh’. The latter two come closest to the Welsh and Irish. By way of the Latin spoken in Roman and sub-Roman Britain it could also have passed into the native vernaculars, thus giving rise to *pwll* and *poll*. Most of the Scottish examples of *poll* in the sense ‘slow-moving stream’ occur in country which either is, or in historical time was, bog-land. Under such circumstances the semantic development from 'marsh, bog' to 'pool in a bog', thence to 'slow-moving stream in bog-land' would have been relatively easy. It might well have taken place while Welsh was still the dominant language in Galloway and the remainder of SW Scotland.

One thing is certain; the initial *p-* shows that Gaelic *poll* does not originate in a Q-Celtic language (Irish or Scots Gaelic) but must be a borrowing, most probably from P-Celtic Welsh.

The usual word for 'burn', 'stream' in Scottish Gaelic, *allt*, denotes a small but rapidly flowing body of water; see, for instance, *bras-shruthain*, 'impetuous torrent', the compound noun applied by the eighteenth-century Gaelic poet, Mac Mhaighstir Alasdair (Alexander MacDonald, c.1700-1770) to *Allt an t-Siùcair*, 'Sugar Burn', in Ardnamurchan. The word has an interesting semantic history. The original significance is indicated by Welsh *allt*, 'hillside', 'steep slope', and Irish *allt*, *ailt*, 'steep-sided glen', 'ravine'. Etymologically the word is related to Latin *altus*, 'high', 'deep'. The transition from 'high (deep) land' to 'steep-sided glen' is easy; the further transition to 'stream running down a steep-sided glen' is only minimally more difficult. Every glen has its stream.

One example of *poll* has already been given, the long and winding **Pultayan Burn**, 278964-287667, Kirkcowan. Of the five remaining, three are in Kirkcowan parish, one in Mochrum and one in Sorbie – all but one, that is to say, in the Moors and all in territory once or still bog-land.

Pulganny Burn, 258770-280749, Kirkcowan. For much of its relatively long and winding course the stream marks a portion of the boundary between Wigtownshire and Carrick. The name is perhaps ironic, *poll gainne*, 'smaller burn'. Maxwell suggests *poll gainmheach*, 'sandy burn', but this is inappropriate for the bog-land through which the burn flows.

Pullower Burn, 226753-218743, Kirkcowan. For part of its length this stream forms the boundary between Wigtownshire and Carrick. It flows into the Tarf. *poll odhar*, 'dun, yellowish burn'.

Polbae Burn. Another long and winding stream, which rises at **The Lodens**, 250720, Kirkcowan (*lodan*, 'little pool', with English *-s* plural added), and eventually, 278728, flows into the Bladnoch; it is probably *poll beithe*, 'birch burn'. **Polbae**, 280730, habitation, Kirkcowan, stands on the left bank of the stream at its lowest reaches.

Pulnasky Burn, 277511-264503, Mochrum: *poll nan ascan*, 'burn of the newts' or 'of the adders'; *asc* has both meanings. The stream begins in moderately high bog-land, but enters Luce Bay by way of a waterfall, **The Grey Mare's Tail**, 265504.

Palmallet, 479422, Sorbie, habitation; *RMS* ii, 839, 11 July 1465, *Powmalate*; 2108, 24 July 1492, *Polmalot*; iii, 3052, 1 February 1545, *Polmaillate*; **Palmallet Loch**, 479424; **Palmallet Point**, 482481. This may be *poll mailleid*, 'slowness burn'. On the basis of seventeenth-century spellings with an intruded *-r-*, Maxwell suggests *poll malairt*, 'barter pool', but the lack of *-r-* in the early forms, as in the modern, argues against this. Palmallet Loch is essentially a large pond, and so *poll* may be 'pool' rather than 'burn'. If so, the second element may not be *mailleid*, but *maladh*, 'bag, satchel': 'bag pool', referring to the shape of the loch.

I have noted only one instance of *allt*, **Alticry**, 280499, Mochrum, habitation; *RMS* iv, 2208, 19 March 1574, *Altnecray*; 2285, 20 July 1574, *Altacray*; Pont, *Aldchry*. It stands beside the lower reaches of **Alticry Burn**, 291506-271497, which runs into Luce Bay under **Alticry Bridge**, 272497. In the immediate vicinity are **Essan Wood**, 282501, and **Alt Wood**, 278500.

The likeliest interpretation is *allt nan craobh*, 'burn of the trees', 'tree-lined burn'. *Essan* in **Essan Wood** is *easan*, 'little waterfall'; at this point there is a cascade in the burn, which is fairly rapid. **Alt Wood** is probably 'burn wood', 'wood by the burn'. Although less likely, it is still possible, that *allt* means 'glen' – in other words that the Gaelic of Wigtownshire here follows the Irish rather than the Scots pattern.

(f) Fal-, Fel-, Phil-: Gaelic *fàl*, 'turf-dyke, hedge, pen-fold for strayed cattle or sheep'

Almost certainly *fàl* is a borrowing, by way of Welsh *gwawl* (obsolete in the modern language), of Latin *vallum*. The latter is a collective noun,

Looking south from Cruggleton Castle; Palmallet Point, White Port, Shaddock Point and Cairn Head

based on *vallus*, ‘stake, pale’, with the basic meaning ‘collection of stakes (arranged to form a barrier)’, hence ‘fence’. Roman military encampments were defended by erecting such fences on a turf foundation. The term *vallum* then became extended to include the foundation as well as the fence; so emerged the general sense ‘wall’. In the Celtic languages a frequent reference is to a hedge or turf wall marking a boundary. The eastern boundary of the old parish of Kinneil, for instance, in West Lothian is situated at the end of the Roman Antonine Wall (NT 014815); the oldest form of the name is *Penguaul*, Welsh *pen*, ‘head, end’, + *gwawl*, ‘(turf-) wall’, whereas the modern form preserves the Gaelic cognates, *ceann*, ‘head, end’, + *fàl*, ‘(turf-)wall’. See MacDonald 1941, 30-31. The Antonine Wall is, of course, constructed of turf.

In later usage the reference is still often to a turf wall or dyke, in terms of Scots a ‘fail dyke’, marking a boundary. Sometimes it is to a hedge, serving the same purpose. In Irish ‘hedge’ is the dominant meaning, but ‘wall’ is fairly frequent, usually signifying a turf wall. Other senses developed, for instance, ‘pound, pen-fold for strayed cattle or sheep’. Maxwell translates, a little inadequately, as *fauld*, ‘fold, pen’, ‘a small field’.

DOST is probably wrong in its suggestion that *fàl* is a derivative of Scots *fail*. The description of Scottish Gaelic *fàl* as ‘not found in Irish’ is demonstrably false – it occurs in the earliest Irish writings and is reasonably frequent in Irish place-names; see *DIL*, s.v. 1 *fál*; Joyce 1871, 216-17, 1913, 348-9.

Fàl, like its Latin antecedent, was originally neuter in gender. On the disappearance of the neuter in Irish, it became masculine. There is a suggestion in the Wigtownshire evidence that sometimes at least it became feminine.

I have an impression that *fàl* appears more often in Galloway place-names than in those from other parts of Scotland. It is particularly frequent in Mochrum parish, but whether this is coincidence or there is some deeper reason, I am unable to say. I have usually rendered the word as ‘turf-dyke’.

Falwhirne, 291715, Kirkcowan: *fàl a’ chuirn*, ‘turf-dyke of the cairn’.

Faldarroch, 368509, Mochrum, habitation: *fàl daraich*, 'oak-tree turf-dyke'.

Falcumnor, 367503, Mochrum, habitation: second element obscure.

Philgown, 367494, Mochrum, habitation: *fàl gobhain*, 'blacksmith's turf-dyke' or *fàl gabhainn*, 'stirks' turf-dyke'. The latter sense is perhaps the more likely.

The latter three places lie almost in a straight line to the west of the modern **Kildarroch** farms. Together they may mark the western boundary of the original holding.

Felyennan, 352460, Mochrum, habitation: second element obscure

Maxwell lists several other names which I have not been able to find on the modern OS map.

Falready, Penninghame: *fàl réitich* (Irish *réidhtig*, from *réidh*, 'clearing, plain'), 'turf-dyke of the level place, plain'.

Falclintalloch, Mochrum: *fàl cluaine tulaich*, 'turf-dyke of hillock-meadow', or possibly, *fàl glin tulaich*, ''turf-dyke of hillock-glen'.

Falnear, Mochrum: *fàl an èarra*, 'turf-dyke of the boundary', 'boundary turf-dyke'.

Falyouse, Mochrum: *fàl dheas*, 'right-hand (i.e., 'southern') turf-dyke'.

Philbains, Mochrum: perhaps *fàl bàin*, 'turf-dyke of the fallow ground', with English plural -*s* added.

Falsheuchan, Kirkinner: *fàl suidheachain*, 'turf-dyke of the bench, ledge', i.e., 'of the level shelf on a hill-side, where one would naturally rest'.

Falwhistle, Kirkinner: Maxwell suggests *fàl iseal*, 'low-lying turf-dyke'. This is possible, but phonetically *fàl uasal* seems better. This might mean no more than 'high turf-dyke', but might better be interpreted as 'enclosure sacred to the fairies', the latter ultimately being the Tuatha Dé Danann of Irish mythology. Cf. Fairy Park, a field-name in Kirkmaiden parish, 094416.

Falwheepan, Glasserton: *fàl a' ghuibin*, 'turf-dyke of the little point' (*guibean*, diminutive of *gob*, 'beak, bill, point'; cf. Gobawhilkin and

Gabarunning, 088370, 089339, Kirkmaiden, and Gabsnout, 181605, Old Luce; (MacQueen 2002, 21).

Falhar, Whithorn: *fàl shiar*, 'western turf-dyke'.

Philwhinnie, Whithorn: *fàl bhinneach*, 'pinnacled, hilly turf-dyke'.

(g) Other names

Blanyvaird, 308763, Penninghame; **Blanyvaird Loch**, 308761: *blèan a' bhaird*, 'the bard's tongue of land', referring to the area enclosed by the course of the **Carrick Burn**, marking the boundary between Wigtownshire and Carrick, from **Loch Dornal**, 297761, (*dornail*, 'of pebbles, handstones', found on the margins of the loch) to **Carrick Mill**, 311760. Compare *Dervaird*, 224584, Old Luce, *doire a' bhaird*, 'the bard's oak-grove', some twelve miles distant as the crow flies. It is uncertain whether a single, or two separate household bards are intended.

There is also another possibility. Halfway between the two is **Finn's Grave**, 243725, Kirkcowan, commemorating the central figure in the Ossianic cycle of Gaelic heroic poems and tales, Fionn mac Cumhaill. Fionn's history was preserved in poems and tales usually attributed to his son, the warrior-bard Oisín (Ossian), and became localised in different parts of the Gaelic-speaking world. In Ireland he is said to have been killed at Áth Brea, Co. Meath, on the River Boyne, and buried on Slieve Gullion, J 0320, Co. Armagh. In Scotland he is said to have been killed on an island in Loch Iubhair, near Benmore, NN 576326, Perthshire, and buried at Killin, probably in the stone circle by the riverside there, NN 576326. The *-in* of Killin, *cill Fhinn*, certainly commemorates a Fionn, although probably a churchman rather than a pagan hero. Sometimes, however, the two become confused.

It is possible that Ossianic legends were also relocated in Gaelic-speaking Galloway and that the bard of Blanyvaird and Dervaird is Oisín son of Fionn. Craigdermott Hill, 071447, Ardwell, 50m., above Ardwell Bay may, for instance, mark a spot where it was told that the lovers, Diarmaid and Grainne, rested during their flight from Grainne's wronged husband, Fionn. The hill itself is not rocky, as Craig- would suggest, but beneath it, on a rocky promontory above the sea, is Doon Castle, 066477, last remnant of a broch in which the pair might have found temporary refuge. In nearby Carrick, Kilphin (High and Laigh Kilphin, 107806, 100809) has the same etymology as Killin.

Slane Fauld, 248729, Kirkcowan: a hybrid. The first element is probably *slàine*, which means 'convalescence' in Scottish Gaelic, but 'health' in Irish. In Ireland it seems to have developed a more particular meaning, 'health-bestowing well'; cf. Slanes, the name of a parish in the Ards of Co. Down. Here too the reference may be to a healing well.

The second element is Scots *fauld*, 'an enclosure for cattle, sheep, or other domestic animals; an enclosed piece of ground used for cultivation, a small field' (*DOST*).

The Lodens, 250720, Kirkcowan; **Loden Moss**, 253718; **Lodens Burn**, 2571: *lodan*, diminutive of *lod*, 'pool, marsh': 'little pool, marsh', with suffixed English plural *-s*.

East Dian, 258707, Kirkcowan, 190 m.: *daigheann*, 'stronghold, fortress', preceded by English 'East'; cf. **Drumadien**, above, c.5 (f).

Tocher Knowes, 251697, Kirkcowan, 185 m.: *tóchar*, 'causeway'. Watson, (Watson 1926, 486) observes that this word 'does not seem to occur in the area that is now Gaelic speaking', but quotes examples from Perthshire and Aberdeenshire, together with Duntocher, NS 4873, Dumbarton, on the Antonine Wall, where 'the causeway was the ancient Roman road'. The word survives in Irish. Cf. **Tacher Wood**, 457462, below.

Urrall, 292696, Kirkcowan, habitation; *RMS* iv, 30, 13 November 1546, *Urrull*; Pont, *Vrrall*; **Urrall Loch**, 286697; **Urrall Fell**, 288701, 184 m.: *ùrla*, literally 'hair', 'lock of hair', applied metaphorically to 'long hair-like grass growing in a marshy or sedgy place' (Joyce 1971, 339). Dwelly gives as a secondary meaning in Scottish Gaelic 'place lying low among hills' – a place in which such grass is likely to grow. This is the most plausible interpretation of the name.

Final unstressed *-a* has been dropped in pronunciation; the second vowel in the forms quoted is epenthetic.

Fleuch Larg Plantation, 364683, Penninghame; *fliuch làirig*, 'wet moor', 'wet pass'.

Dronan Hill, 383618, Penninghame, 57 m.: *dronnan*, 'ridge, hump'.

Craighlaw, 306611, Kirkcowan, habitation; *RMS* ii, 731, 14 July 1459, 732; 1459, 2251, 22 October 1500; 3042, 30 January 1507, *Crachlew*; Pont, *Craichlaw*; **Craighlaw Mains**, 309609; **Craighlaw Loch**, 309611; **Craighlaw Wood**, 306613; **Craighlaw Bridge** (where A75 crosses small stream), 302614: obscure; possibly *crèach leamh*, 'elm underwood'.

Clary, 424604, Penninghame, habitation; Pont, *Clary*; **Clary Height**, 421606; 37 m.; **Carse of Clary**, 425602, habitation: Maxwell plausibly suggests *clèirigh*, 'clergy'. Alexander Gordon (c. 1516-1575), Bishop of Whithorn from 1559 and titular Archbishop of Athens, died at Clary, leaving the property to his daughter Barbara, wife of Anthony Stewart, parson of Penninghame. At this time Clary clearly had church connections with Whithorn. It is not likely, however, that the name was given as late as the second half of the sixteenth century; connections were probably already in existence much earlier.

Crosherie, **West**, 330600, Kirkcowan, habitation; **East**, 334597, habitation; *RMS* ii, 3294, 25 January 1508, *Uvicrossery* (*Uvir Crossery*), *Nethir Crossery*; Pont, *O*[*vir*} *Kroshary* (close to a bridge across the Tarf), *N*[*ethir*] *Chroishary*: *crosaire*, 'crossroads', 'often applied to the junction of three roads' (Dinneen). The reference here may be to the crossing of the Tarf.

Gass, 335578, Kirkcowan, habitation; *RMS* ii, 2520, 14 February 1500, *Gas*; 2578, 22 March 1501, *Gass*; 3294, 29 January 1508, *Gasse*; Pont, *Gaiss*; **Gass Wood**, 339577: *gas*, coppice, copse'.

The root meaning of *gas* is 'sprig, shoot, twig', from which develops the secondary meaning 'a small wood or thicket consisting of underwood and small trees grown for the purpose of periodic cutting' (*OED*). The cuttings might be used for firewood or for basket-work, or the manufacture of wattle for fences etc. There is another Gass, 244644, and Gass Farm, 241640, in New Luce parish, in the immediate vicinity of Tor Wood, 244643, and Derwindle Hill, 250642, 102 m., *doire bhinndeil*, 'thicket of the swaddling cloth', perhaps indicating that the trees and bushes grew uncommonly thick on the hill.

Lurg Hill, 384555, Wigtown, 29 m.: *lorg*, 'leg, shank, shin', referring to the shape of the hill.

Tahall ('house of the rugged bank') Mains

Standing Stones of Chilcarroch, 'hump of the standing stones'. The 'boundary ridge' is in the background.

Crouse, 364553, Kirkinner, habitation; Pont, *Kreochs*; **Crouse Cottages**, 367552; **Crouse Moor**, 3554; **Crouse Burn**: *cruadhas*, *cruas*, 'hardship', abstract from *cruaidh*, 'hard, difficult, painful' – presumably the tenants' comment on the land.

Clutag, **North**, 382532, Kirkinner, habitation; **South**, 378520, habitation; *RMS* ii, 3018, 23 December 1506, *Cloidoog*; Pont, *Cloutaig*; **Clutag Fauld**, 382514, 57 m.: *clùdag*, 'little patch', diminutive of *clùd*, 'patch, rag, clout', a borrowing into Gaelic of Scots *cloot*, 'patch, piece of cloth'. Again probably the tenants' comment on the holding.

Scots *fauld*, as above, under **Slane Fauld**.

Tahall (stress on second syllable) **Mains**, 401522, Kirkinner, habitation; Ainslie 1782, *Tachall croft*; **Little Tahall**, 400525, habitation: *taigh* [*na*] *h-aill*, 'house of the rugged bank, rough steep' (see illustration).

Clantibuies, 335516, Mochrum, habitation; *RMS* iv, 2208, 19 March 1574, *Clontagbuis*; 2285, 20 July 1574, *Clontagboy*: *clann Aodha buì*, 'family of Yellow-Haired Hugh'; cf. Clandeboy, 3437, Co. Down. 'The name Clandeboy originally applied to a sept descended from Yellow-Haired Hugh of Tyrone, who died in 1283. It was later applied to a large territory in south Antrim and north Down which was settled by this sept in the 14th century' (McKay 1999, 41). Members of this sept must have settled at Clantibuies, probably during the 14th or 15th century.

Chilcarroch, 350498, Mochrum, habitation; *RMS* iv, 350, 17 July 1549, *Challinearrich*; 764, 28 February 1553, *Schallochquharroch*; Pont, *Chalkarrach*; **Chilcarroch Loch**, 356498: A difficult name. It is to be assumed that the *-e-* in RMS iv, 350, is a mistranscription of *-c-*, and that the *Schalloch-* of 764 is a wild attempt at an etymology. *Ch-* usually represents Gaelic *T-* before a front vowel; the first element may therefore be *tel* or *til*, variant forms of *tul,* 'protuberance, projecting part', also 'forehead', here applied metaphorically to a natural feature of the landscape. If the *-in-* of Challinearrich represents *na*, genitive plural of the definite article, the second element is likely to be *carragh*, 'standing stone': *til* [*na*] [*g*]*carragh*, 'hump of the standing stones'. There are standing stones on the top of the nearby **Shaw Hill**, 347499, 106 m., probably the original 'hump'; see illustration.

Drungarron House, 482481, Sorbie, habitation: *dronn garrain*, 'underwood ridge'.

Sanquhar Hill, 419478, Sorbie, 68 m.: *seanchathair*, 'old fort'. There is no indication of a fort at this site.

Changue, 296477, Mochrum, habitation; Pont, *Chang*; **Changue Cottage South**, 300474, habitation; **Changue Wood**, 303486; **Changue Burn**: *teanga*, 'tongue', referring to **Changue Fell**, 306496, 187 m., and **Bennan Hill** (*beannan*, 'little hill, peak', diminutive of *beann*, 'top, peak'), 296489, 159 m., which together form a ridge, a tongue of land, towards Luce Bay.

Druchtag (stressed on first syllable), 349473, Mochrum, habitation; *RMS* iv, 1173, 16 May 1557, *Mekill Drochtaig*; 2285, 29 July 1574, *Litill Drochtaig*, *Dreuchdag*, *Drochdag*; Pont, *Dreugtak*; **Druchtag Cottage**, 351474, habitation; **Druchtag Mote Hill**, 349467: *drochaideag*, 'little bridge' (diminutive of *drochaid*, 'bridge'). The site of the actual bridge, and the name of the stream which it crossed, are both unclear; the stream was probably the **Killantrae Burn**.

Lenrohmas, 375468, Kirkinner, habitation: obscure; perhaps *lèana ròmais*, 'meadow of hairiness', 'hairy meadow'. *Lèana* implies a field of luxuriant grass, which might be described as 'hairy'.

Tacher Wood, 457462, Sorbie; **Tacher Bridge** (over **Kilfillan Burn**), 457466; **Tacher Hill**, 459459, 35 m.: *tóchar*, 'causeway'; see above **Tocher Knowes**, 251697. The causeway is now represented by the minor road from **Broughton Mains**, 452451, to **Hillside Cottages**, 458468.

Clone, **High**, 339457, Mochrum, habitation; **Low**, 336452, habitation; *RMS* iv, 1173, 16 May 1557, *Cloyne*; Pont, *Cloyin*; **Clone Bridge** (on A747, over **Clone Burn**), 333449; **Clone Point**, 331450: *cluain*, 'meadow' (probably along Clone Burn).

Ringan, 487453, Sorbie: *rinnin*, 'little promontory', diminutive of *rinn*, 'point, promontory. The modern spelling has been influenced by the proper name 'Ringan', a form of 'Ninian'.

Grennan, 413452, Glasserton, habitation; **Grennan Hill**, 412453, 66 m.; **Grennan Moss**, 4045: *grianan*, 'sunny spot', 'place where peats are dried'. The name is widespread; cf. MacQueen 2002, 68-9.

Cults, 461435, Sorbie, habitation; *RMS* ii, 87, 18 March 1426, *Qwyltis*; iii, 501, 5 October 1527, *Quyltis*; iv, 240, 1 August 1548, *Qwiltis*; 871, 4 December 1553, *Quiltis*: *coillte* (*caillti*), older Irish plural of *coille*, 'a wood', with English plural -*s* added: 'woods', 'woodlands'. The name is widespread in Scotland; cf., e.g., Cults, 122596, Inch, habitation; Cults, NJ 9103, near Aberdeen, also Cult, NS 926640, Whitburn, West Lothian, where no -*s* has been added. There are now no woodlands in the immediate neighbourhood.

Dowies, 381430, Glasserton, habitation: *dubh ais*, 'black moss', 'black marshy ground'.

Kevans, 467422, Sorbie, habitation: *cabhan*, 'field, plain', earlier 'hollow, cavity, valley, hollow plain', with English plural -*s* added. The modern farm stands on a ridge at a height of 46 m.; the name refers primarily to the surrounding lands. Cf. **Kevan Braes**, 446397, Whithorn, 72 m.

Lagtutor Hill, 359412, Glasserton, 48 m.: *lag an t-sudaire*, 'the tanner's hollow' or 'the shoe-makers hollow'. Presumably the hollow was under the hill.

Dinnans, 474409, Whithorn, habitation; Pont, *Dounen*: **Dinnans Hill**, 471406, 37 m.; **Dinnans Cottage**, 472406, habitation: *dùnain* (diminutive of *dùn*, 'fort'), 'little fort', with English plural or possessive -*s* added. There is no fort in the vicinity; *dùnain* may have come to mean no more than 'little hill'.

Claywhippart Bridge (over the **Stirnie Birnie Burn**, just above its junction with the **Ket**), 455404, Whithorn: *cladh thiobairt*, 'well-churchyard', i.e. 'churchyard with a (holy) well'; alternatively 'well-mound' or 'well-ditch'. The first is the most probable. The bridge is immediately to the east of Whithorn, where one might expect to find a burial place.

Catyans, 437403, Whithorn, habitation: *coitcheann*, 'common grazing' (for the burgesses of Whithorn), with English -*s* plural added.

Skeog, Low, 459402, Whithorn, habitation; **High**, 454396, habitation; **Skeog Cottage**, 459407; Pont, *Skioch*: *sgìtheog*, 'hawthorn'.

High Rouchan, 411388, Glasserton, habitation; Pont, *Rouchan*, habitation; **Rouchan Hill**, 417392, 97 m.; **Rouchan Fey Plantation**,

407382; **Rouchan Pond**, 411382: Maxwell suggests Irish Gaelic *ruadhán*, 'reddish land'. Possibly the original name of **Glasserton Home Farm,** 417379, was Rouchan.

Claymoddie, 421378, Glasserton, habitation; 425378, habitation; Pont, *Clymady*: *cladh madaidh*, 'dog's, wolf's or fox's trench'.

Drury Lane, 433378, Glasserton, habitation; Ainslie 1782, *Drury Lane*: the reference to London's theatre district is obvious but somewhat obscure. Maxwell explains it thus: 'A modern and quasi-humorous adaptation of *dobharach*, *dúrach*, meaning wet land, with Lowland Scottish *lane*, a slow-running stream, added. This exactly describes the place'.

Machermore's Mill Stone, 395376, Glasserton, a name for the steep, rocky northern face of **Fell of Carleton**, 130 m.: *machair m*[*h*]*or*, 'big fertile plain'. The implication is that a very large area of arable ground would be needed to produce enough grain for this enormous mill stone to grind.

Doon, 460372, Glasserton, habitation: *dùn*, 'fort'. The reference is to **Doon of Arbrack**, 457373; see below, chapter 7.

Laggan Camp (Iron Age fortification), 398371, Glasserton; Pont, *Laggan*, habitation: *lagan*, 'little hollow'.

Leakin Hill, 463365, Whithorn, 57 m.: for *Leakin* Maxwell suggests *leacann*, 'broad slope, steep shelving ground'.

Cutreoch, 466357, Whithorn, habitation; Pont, *Cettreoch*; **Cutreoch Cottage**, 466359, habitation: The first element is difficult, perhaps *cuid*, 'share', alternatively a Gaelic adaptation of Scots *cot*, 'cottage'. The second element is the surname Reach, Reoch, Riach, from Gaelic *riabhach*, 'brindled, greyish': 'Reach's share' or 'Reach's cottage'. Pont's form suggests that the first element is *cuid.*

An riabhach mór, 'the big grizzled one' means 'the Devil'. It is thus possible that **Cutreoch** means 'the Devil's portion'.

The image on Pont's map suggests that in his time Cutreoch was a substantial mansion.

Tonderghie, 442355, Whithorn, habitation; Pont, *Tonreghe*; **Tonderghie Cottages**, 444355, habitation: *tón ri gaoith*, 'arse to wind'. Cf. *Tandragee Hill*, 052519, Stoneykirk, 128 m. The name is also found in

Ireland, e.g., *Tandragee*, 3034, Co. Armagh.

Lobbocks, 432352, Glasserton: *lobaig* (diminutive pl. from *lob*, 'puddle'), 'little puddles', with English plural -*s* added.

Cutcloy, 452350, Whithorn, habitation; Pont, *Cotclay*; **Cutcloy Cottages**, 452350: *cuid*, 'share', or *cot*, 'cottage', followed by the surname [Mac]Cloy, '[son of] Lewis': 'MacCloy's share', or, in view of Pont's form, more probably, '[Mac]Cloy's cottage'.

Chapter 7

Scandinavian (Norse) Names

Some account of the Scandinavian element in Wigtownshire place-names to the west of the Moors and Machars will be found in MacQueen 2002, 86-90 (I should like to add Swinefell, 253540, Old Luce, habitation: ON *svína fjall*, 'swine-hill', probably 'hill where swine feed'). To a surprising extent, names in the Moors and Machars differ, in number as in other ways. If we include partly-Scandinavian inversion compounds in Kirk- and Carse-, there are 26 Scandinavian names in the Moors and Machars, as opposed to 31 in the smaller area of the Rhinns and Luce Valley. The main defining elements also differ; to the west we have *völlr*, 'field' and *vík*, 'bay', to the east, *bœr/byr*, 'fermtoun' and *dalr*, 'dale, valley'. Although I should personally be inclined to consider *völlr* (and *akr*, as in *Stennaker*, 'Stoneykirk') as habitation names proper, only *bœr/byr*, is generally so regarded, and it is confined to the Moors and Machars. This is sometimes classified as Danish (*byr*) rather than Norse (*bœr*); Gillian Fellows-Jensen, for instance, remarks that 'The names recorded in south-west Scotland ... resemble in type the *bý*-names of the Danelaw and Denmark much more closely than the *bœr*-names of the Northern and Western Isles' and adds that 'the distribution of names in -*bý* in south-west Scotland suggests that Dumfriesshire was settled by Scandinavians coming from south and south-east of the Solway and from across the English border rather than from across the Irish Sea, while the *bý*-names in the lowlands of Kirkcudbrightshire and Wigtownshire would seem to mark an extension westward' (Fellows-Jensen in Oram and Stell 1991, 83, 84). It seems to me that, for the Wigtownshire names at least, another opinion is possible. Fellows-Jensen makes no mention of the many names in *bœr* (some of them inversion compounds) found in the Isle of Man, the ultimate source of which is certainly not the English Danelaw.

The -*r* in *bœr* and *byr*, incidentally, is there merely as an ending for the nominative case. In the oblique cases it disappears. Place-names very seldom are used in the nominative; it is the form for the other cases which has survived.

Names in Kirk- and Carse- have already been discussed. This chapter deals with the relatively small number of purely Scandinavian names, that is, names given by speakers of a Scandinavian language unaffected by the Gaelic or Welsh of their neighbours. They were not necessarily dominant in their neighbourhood. One name, **Sorbie**, 436467, Sorbie, gave its name to a parish, but this, probably, was at a relatively late date; two smaller parishes, one, **Kirkmadrine**, an inversion-compound, the other, ***Kilfillan***, purely Gaelic, were combined to form the new, larger parish. Two other sites, **Eggerness**, 492477, Sorbie, habitation, and **Arbrack**, 450371, Glasserton, habitation, belong to places of some natural strength, exploited, however, at a much earlier period, during the Iron Age. There is no particular suggestion that Vikings used them as strongholds.

In other parts of Britain and Ireland, churches often became the target of Viking attacks, but Whithorn seems to be an exception. The wooden minster there was destroyed by fire in the mid-ninth century but there is no evidence that this was caused by a raid. 'The burning of the buildings at Whithorn could have resulted from an unrecorded Viking incursion, the imperfectly documented raid of Alpín [see MacQueen 2002, 13-14], the vengeance of his son Cinéad [Kenneth], or a hypothetical Northumbrian civil war; it could equally have been an accident' (Hill 1997, 22). Whithorn was a well-known place. The lack of witness for the first four suggests the last as the most probable explanation.

Indeed, some Norse-speakers may have reached the Machars more as refugees than conquerors. Under the year 902 the Annals of Ulster record that 'The Heathens [Vikings] were driven from Ireland, i.e. from the fortress of Áth Cliath [Dublin] , by Mael Finnia son of Flannacán with the men of Brega [the district north of Dublin] and Cerball son of Muiricán with the Laigin [the men of Leinster south of Dublin]; and they abandoned a good number of their ships, and escaped half-dead after they had been wounded and broken' (*AU*, *s.a.* 902). Much Scandinavian settlement around the eastern fringes of the Irish Sea has been traced back to this and subsequent activities by Irish kings, culminating in the battle of Clontarf (1014), which saw the end of independent Scandinavian power in Ireland.

All in all, it looks as if the Scandinavians arrived peacefully, rather than as invaders or conquerors, and as if they formed a minority of the population.

The Scandinavians in Dublin and towns like Waterford and Limerick were traders. The Solway Firth was the highway by which they maintained contact with settlements in Britain, particularly Scandinavian York. Norse place-names seem to indicate something of the route followed and the harbours used. The word *nes*, 'cape, headland', plays a significant role, whether in isolation or in combination with other place-name elements. In the Machars, for instance, we have **Egger*ness***, 492477, Sorbie, and **Skellarie Rock**, 450513, Kirkinner, both close to what Pont calls **The Roade of Innerwell** in Wigtown Bay. *Roade* is used in the sense 'a sheltered piece of water near the shore where vessels may lie at anchor in safety; a roadstead' (*OED*); see above, chapter 2. The shelter was provided by Egger*ness* and the rock was dangerous for approaching ships or for any that had lost their moorings. To the south, **Eggerness Point**, 493463, Sorbie, and **Dumbie Point**, 486460, Sorbie (also perhaps a Scandinavian name), flank the approach to **Garlieston Bay**, another good harbour. In the Rhinns, Caillie*ness* Point, 153357, Kirkmaiden, provides shelter, from the south to Crawar, Cairngarroch and Drummore Bays, from the north to Maryport Bay. In the regality of Glenluce, the Mull of Sinni*ness*, 227516, Old Luce, provides shelter, from the north to Auchenmalg Bay, from the south to Stairhaven and the mouths of the Luce and Piltanton. In the Stewartry, Almor*ness* Point, 840515, Buittle, protects Auchencairn Bay and Orchardton Bay to the west, the Urr estuary to the east. Souther*ness* Point, 979540, Kirkbean, marks the entry to safe harbour in the Nith estuary. All these names, I suggest, have their origin in sea-traffic, mainly from and to Dublin. Cargoes, it seems likely, were finally unloaded at Port Carlisle, NY 241622, Cumberland, sheltered by Bow*ness*-on-Solway, 224629, for transport by land through the Eden valley and Stainmore to the Vale of York. Skinbur*ness*, NY 207558, is also on the Solway coast of Cumberland; it may originally have sheltered a harbour on the estuary of the river Waver and indicate a more southerly route for shipping.

In the preceding paragraph, the phrase '*Mull* of Sinniness' is worth noting. The hill above Almorness Point is called Moyl (837515, Buittle). In MacQueen 2002, 14, I took 'Mull' in 'Mull of Galloway', 155304, Kirkmaiden, to be Gaelic *maol*, 'cape, promontory'. More probably, as it now seems to me, it represents ON *múli*, 'muzzle, snout', but also 'projecting mountain, "mull"'. The same etymology applies to the Mull of Logan, 075418, Kirkmaiden, the Mull of Sinniness and to Moyl (also to the Mull of Kintyre, NR 589071, Southend, Argyll, and the Mull of Oa, NR 269415, Kildalton and Oa, Islay. Hiberno-Norse trade-routes also extended northwards into the Firth of Clyde and the Hebrides; cf., e.g., Skip*ness* Point, NR 912572, Sadell and Skipness, Argyll.

Múli was a term used to indicate places of danger as well as safe harbours. The tidal rips around the Mull of Galloway make it a mark for seamen, but also a place to avoid. There are similar rips around the Mull of Logan, but it also shelters two good harbours, Port Nessock and Port Gill Bays. 'Nessock' is O.N. *nasa vík*, 'inlet of the noses', i.e., the two headlands which define the bay, the Mull of Logan to the north and Cairniewellan Head to the south. Both these may originally have had Scandinavian names; the old farm which stands above Cairniewellan Head is called *Mul*daddie.

Another element which seems to fit the pattern is ON *sker*, 'rock in the sea, skerry', found, for instance, in **The Scares** (Scaurs), 256333-264345, dangerous rocks in Luce Bay between Rhinns and Machars, and also a sanctuary for many birds, especially gannets, which were probably hunted. The Scar, 0467, Kirkcolm, is a string of rocks in Loch Ryan marking the seaward limit of The Wig, 0367-0467, ON *vík*, 'inlet, bay', a sheltered anchorage. The sand and mud banks on both sides of the Solway are littered with rocks in the names of which the word Scar appears – towards the north shore, Rough Scar, NY 103632, for instance, and Brewing Scar, NY 124635; towards the south, Herdhill Scar, NY 212626, and High West Scar, NY 188618, both the latter in the vicinity of Bowness-on-Solway.

All this may seem to take us a long way from the Machars. It does, however, indicate that sea-borne trade was probably instrumental in at least some instances of Scandinavian settlement. Sorbie, for one, may originally have been a self-sufficient trading station, far enough from the coast to be reasonably secure from piratic incursion, but, for the receipt of trade-goods, still reasonably near Garlieston Bay and The Road of Innerwell.

Most Scandinavian names belong to the Whithorn Machars (see above, chapter 1). Two, **Bysbie Cottage**, 470360, Whithorn, and **Bysbie Mill**, 476366, refer to a bishop, presumably the bishop of Whithorn. The lands of Bysbie, it would seem, were situated around the harbour at Isle of Whithorn. By the tenth century many Scandinavians settled in Ireland and elsewhere had converted to Christianity. The Scandinavians of Bysbie may have used their ships in the service of the church at Whithorn.

(a) Names in –bie, -by, Old Norse *bœr*/Old Danish *byr*, 'fermtoun'

Dorbie Wood, 347628, Penninghame: Apart from this name, I have no evidence of the existence of a fermtoun called Dorbie. The name, however, closely resembles Derby in the English Danelaw, SK 3533, and the Manx Jurby, SC 355983, Michael, in Norse territory: perhaps O.N. *diur bœr*, 'fermtoun where deer were seen'.

Sorbie, 436467, Sorbie, habitation; **Sorbie Tower**, 451470, habitation; Pont, *Soirbuy*; **Sorbie Farm**, 456478, habitation; *Dryburgh Liber*, c. 1200, *Sowerby*; 1282, *Sowrby*; *RMS* i, Appendix 1, 20, 101, reign of Robert I, 1306-29, *Soreby*, *Soureby*: ON *saurr*, 'mud, dirt' + *bœr*, 'fermtoun', 'muddy, dirty fermtoun'. Saurbœr in Iceland was so called because the district around was boggy. The same is true of Sorbie.

The name occurs three times in Denmark. In the Machars, however, it seems more likely to be Norse than Danish. No instance of the name occurs in the predominantly Danish territory of the English Five Boroughs, Leicester, Lincoln, Nottingham, Stamford and Derby. Outside this area, the name is found in Iceland, in Argyll, NM 195533, Tiree, NL 989425, Coll, NM 863287, Oban; Ayrshire NS 247444; Fife, NO 538088, Cameron; Dumfriesshire, NY 3785, Ewes; Cumberland; Westmorland, NY 7762, 6128; Lancashire, SD4738, 2173; Yorkshire, SE 4480, 0621; Isle of Man, SC 212708. Like the territory of the Five Boroughs, Yorkshire was largely settled by Danes, although, for much of the tenth century, they lived under the domination of a Norse aristocracy. The other areas, with the possible

Sorbie ('muddy, dirty fermtoun'), c.1870. Notice the flat bogland behind.

Sorbie Tower today

exception of Fife, were predominantly Norse.

Dumbie Point, 486460, Sorbie: There is no certainty that this name refers to a lost fermtoun. It bears some resemblance to Dounby, HY 2819, Birsay, Orkney. On this Marwick comments: 'A puzzling name. The ending suggests an ON *bœr*, 'farm', but as I have seen no mention of the name in old records, its origins must be regarded as doubtful' (Marwick 1952, 157).

Appleby, 411409, Glasserton, habitation; *RMS* iv, 2823, 1 January 1579, *Apilvie*; Pont *Apleby*: ON *epli bœr*, 'apple fermtoun'. ON *epli* may have been replaced by OE *æppel*, 'apple'. There are English parallels, one, NY 6820, in Westmorland, and thus probably Norse, one, SE 9313, in Lincolnshire, and one, SK 3109, in Leicestershire, the latter two both in the Danish territory of the Five Boroughs.

Bysbie Cottage, 470360, Whithorn, habitation; **Bysbie Mill**, 476366: in these 'the first element appears to be ON *biskup*, "bishop"' (Fellows-Jensen in Oram and Stell 1991, 84-5), referring to the bishop of Whithorn; cf. **Bishopton**, 436411, Whithorn, discussed in chapter 2. The name suggests that the bishopric remained in existence after 900.

Maxwell lists a ***Corsby***, Penninghame, which I have not been able to identify, but which, presumably, is the same as the frequently-occurring Crosby, ON *crossa bœr* or *byr*, 'fermtoun with crosses'. Other examples of the name are to be found in Ayrshire, NS 341302; Berwickshire, NL 5943; Cumberland, NY 0537, 4557; Westmorland, NY 6214, 7609; Lancashire, SH 3199, and the Isle of Man, SC 325792. This distribution approximates to that of Sorbie/Sowerbie.

(b) Names in -dale, ON -*dalr*, 'dale, valley'

Kilquhockadale, 293678, Kirkcowan, habitation: as noted above, chapter 4, the name is a hybrid in which Gaelic *cill Choca*, 'Cuaca's monastic cell or church' has been combined with ON *dalr*. The compound is Norse in form: 'valley of Cuaca's monastic cell'.

Kidsdale, 433366, Glasserton, habitation: Pont, *Kidsdall*: this looks like a compound name, ending in Norse *dalr*. The first element is less certain. In ON 'dale of the kids, young goats' would be *kiðjadalr*, leaving the -*s*- of Kidsdale unexplained. The first element is probably a proper name, perhaps Kjötvi (see *Grettissaga*, 2): 'Kjötvi's valley'.

(c) Other names

The Holm, 346602, Penninghame, habitation: ON *hólmr*, 'a piece of dry land in a fen, a piece of land partly surrounded by streams or by a stream'.The Holm stands on marshy land within the angle of the confluence of Tarf and Bladnoch. Cf. **Holm of Glasnick**, 343632, Penninghame, on the left bank of the Bladnoch.

Skellarie (stress on first syllable) **Rock**, 450513, Kirkinner; Pont *Skellary*, habitation: ON *skeljar eyrr*, 'shell gravel-bank, spit'. The rock is at high-water mark on the shore of Wigtown Bay. Shellfish were used for food and as bait. The discarded shells were used by farmers and others for the production of lime.

Bing Hill, 421500, Kirkinner, 87 m.; **Bing**, 421502, habitation: ON *bingr*, 'heap', also 'bed, bolster'. The reference is to the shape of the hill.

Corwall, 288495, Mochrum, habitation; *RMS* iii, 1912; 10 February 1539, *Corwell*: the second element is probably ON *völlr*, 'field'. The first element may be ON *kjarr*, 'thicket', or else a personal name, Kori or even the Gaelic Corc: 'field of thickets (whin bushes?)', 'Kori's field' or 'Corc's field'.

Eggerness, 492477, Sorbie, habitation; *RMS* ii, 2018, 8 March 1491; 3246, 23 June 1508, *Egirnes*; Pont, *Eggerness*; **Eggerness Castle** (an Iron Age promontory-fort), 494475; **Eggerness Wood**, 487472; **Eggerness Point**, 493463; Pont, *Point of Eggerness*: ON *eggjar nes*, 'edge headland'. Cf. the Manx Agneash, SC 430861, *eggjar nes*, and Gob Ago, Maughold, *eggjar höfoð*, 'edge-how or head', to which *gob*, 'headland', has been prefixed (Kneen 1925, 297).

Arbrack (stress on first syllable), 450371, Glasserton, habitation; *RMS* iii, 729, 16 January 1529, *Arbrok*; iv, 1309, 30 October 1558, *Arbrog*; Pont, *Arbrack*: ON *jarð borg*, 'stronghold (made) of earth' (with metathesis of *-r-* in the second element), the name referring to **Doon of Arbrack**, 459373, now obliterated by a quarry, also commemorated in **Doon**, 460373, habitation, from Gaelic *dùn*, 'fort'.

Physgill House, 427367, Glasserton, habitation; *RMS* ii,

990, n.d.; 1470, 5 April 1481, *Fischgill*; iii, 1848, 24 October 1538; 2508, 19 November 1541, *Fischegill*; Pont, *Phyisgill*; **Physgill Glen**, 425358-432365: ON *fiska gil*, 'fish gully'. Maxwell translates *gil* as 'stream' and comments: 'It is such a small stream that the name seems the reverse of appropriate; but it enters the sea on a beach [**Port Castle Bay**, 425358] – an interval between cliffs – convenient for landing fish from boats'.

Orfasey, 470353, Whithorn, habitation: ON *orfris ey*, 'ebb-isle', i.e. 'an island which is joined to the mainland at low tide'. The name is not appropriate to the site and may well be a modern importation. The south end, however, of the peninsula between Isle of Whithorn and Wigtown Bays once formed such an island, and it is just possible that at some period the name has been transferred from this to the neighbouring site. **Ramsey**, 480359, ON *rams ey*, 'wild-garlic island', is now the name of the most southerly part of the peninsula, but may once have applied to the entire tidal island for which *Orfris ey* was an alternative descriptive name.

Chapter 8

Scots and English Names

(a) Names in *-ton* (*-toun*)

Names of this type which may belong to the OE (Anglian) period have already been discussed in chapter 2. These now listed are no earlier than the thirteenth or fourteenth century; some are demonstrably later.

Shennanton, 342632, Kirkcowan, habitation; Pont, *Schinnentoun*, habitation; **Mark of Shennanton**, 341646, Kirkcowan, habitation: the first element is the old Galloway surname Aschennan, Irish Gaelic *O' Seanáin*, 'descendent of Seanán', a name which is an affectionate diminutive of *sean*, 'the ancient'; 'fermtoun belonging to the descendents of the little ancient one'. The *A-* of Aschennan has been dropped. The first element of the place-name is Gaelic, but formally the name is Scots.

It may be relevant that John Aschennan of Park (188570, Old Luce) appears in charters 1520-72. He, or members of his family, may have farmed Shennanton. Shennan, however, was a relatively common name.

Mark is *march*, 'the boundary(-line) of a property'. Mark of Shennanton began as a subsidiary fermtoun on the northern part of the Shennanton land.

Clugston, 354574, Kirkcowan, habitation; *RMS* ii, 2521, 14 February 1500; 3294, 29 January 1508, *Clugstoun*: The first element appears to be the possessive of a personal name which I have not identified. See also below, **Boreland**, 352583, Kirkcowan, habitation.

Newtonhill, 404527, Kirkinner, habitation: 'hill with a new fermtoun on it'. **Newton Hill**, 400529, 68 m., is nearby. Newtonhill may itself be the new fermtoun, but more probably it is **Little Tahall**, 400525, Kirkinner, with Newtonhill as a later development.

On Ainslie's 1782 map, **Braehead**, 420522, Kirkinner, habitation, is called ***Newtown***. It is about a mile from Newtonhill and may have given rise to the name.

Stewarton, 447497, Kirkinner, habitation; Pont, *Stuartown*:

'fermtoun owned or occupied by people called Stewart or Stuart'. The reference may be to ancestral kinsmen of the local landholder, Sir John Stewart, created Lord Garlies in 1607 and Earl of Galloway in 1623. Cf. **Macher Stewart**, 417461, Sorbie, habitation.

Dowalton, 401458, Sorbie, habitation; Pont, *Dowaltoun*: '[Mc] douall's fermtoun'; **Dowalton Loch** (now drained); **Dowalton Burn**; **Dowalton Hill**, 409461, 70 m.. Joanne Makdowell of Fruich [Freugh, Stoneykirk in the Rhinns] and Dowelstoun, son and heir apparent of Margaret Dunbar, appears as a witness in *RMS* iv, 2285, 20 July 1574. In an earlier charter (RMS iii, 325, 7 July 1525) Thomas Makdowell of **Mindork** (308585, 315590, Kirkcowan) and his spouse Margaret Dunbar, obtained the lands of Stranraer and Markslave in the Rhinns. Thomas probably was John's father. The McDouall's had extensive holdings over much of Wigtownshire.

Two names stand separate from this group. They are later and in them *-ton* signifies 'town' or 'village' rather than 'fermtoun'.

Newton Stewart, 4065, Penninghame, habitation. On 1 July 1677 William Stewart, third son of James, 2nd Earl of Galloway (1610-71), obtained from Charles II a charter for the creation on this site of a burgh of barony, which he named **Newton Stewart**. This was changed to ***Newton Douglas*** by [Sir] William Douglas (d. 1809), who purchased it in 1784 and made considerable additions and improvements (he was also founder of Castle Douglas, 762622, Balmaghie, in the Stewartry). In 1826 the burgh was sold to George Stewart, 8th Earl of Galloway (succeeded 1806, d. 1834), who restored the old name.

Garlieston, 477464, Sorbie, habitation: The village of ***Carswell***, located on the present site of Garlieston, was expanded from the 1740s by Alexander Stewart, Lord Garlies, son of James Stewart, 5th Earl of Galloway, whom he succeeded as 6th Earl in 1746. By 1774 at latest the name had been changed to Garlieston. The village was geometrically planned and formed a port for the Machars and an estate village for Galloway House (Kirkwood 2007, 14).

Carswell may be Norse; *carse* together with *völlr*, 'field', 'field on the bank (? of the **Kilfillan Burn**)'.

(b) Names in *-land*, 'land or lands as property or as a commodity' (*DOST*)

Liberland in **Fell of Eldrig of Liberland**, 249748, Kirkcowan, 202 m.; **Liberland Burn**, 237743-249733: 'land occupied by a libber or gelder (of farm animals)'.

For **Eldrig** see above, chapter 6, (d).

Oldland, 321611, Kirkcowan, habitation: perhaps 'land cultivated for a long time' or 'land formerly cultivated (but now fallen out of use)'. Cf. **Old Lands Wood**, 393520, Kirkinner, and Oldland, Gloucestershire.

Kirkland, 'land belonging to a church', in **Ring and Kirkland**, 338604, Kirkcowan, habitation; Pont, *Kirklant*, habitation; **West Kirkland**, 431568, Wigtown, habitation; **East Kirkland**, 432566, Wigtown, habitation; **Kirkland Hill**, 432558, Wigtown, 76 m.; all derived from Pont, *Kirkland*, habitation; **Kirkland Hill**, 419517, Kirkinner, 53 m.; **Kirkland of Longcastle**, 377473, Kirkinner, habitation, from Pont, *Longcastel k.*; **Kirkland Marsh**, 475425, Sorbie (close to **Cruggleton Church,** 478427, Sorbie; Pont, *Kirck of Cruggeltoun*); **Kirkland**, 418385, Glasserton. The reference in each case is to the local parish church. Both Longcastle and Cruggleton were pre-Reformation parishes.

'Kirk' here is the Scots word for 'church' rather than Norse *kirkja.*

'Ring', in **Ring and Kirkland** is Gaelic *rinn*, 'point, promontory' and refers to the point of land between Bladnoch and Tarf immediately above their junction.

Cotland, 420543, Wigtown, habitation; Pont, *Cotlant*; **Low Cotland**, 423550, Wigtown (now a field-name): '*Cotland*: land attached to a cottage' (*DOST*).

Boreland, 352583, Kirkcowan, habitation; *RMS* ii, 2520, 14 February 1500; 2578, 22 March 1501, *Bordland*; Pont, *Boirland of Kingston*; **Boreland Fell**, 347592, Kirkcowan, 90 m.; **Boreland Terrace**, 418519, Kirkinner, habitation; **Boreland of Longcastle**, 384471, Kirkinner, habitation; *RMS* ii, 2391, 13 March 1498, *Bordland de Longestir*; 2464, 10 November 1498, *Bordland et Park de Longcastill*;

Pont, *Boirland*.

As explained in MacQueen 2002, 20, *Boreland* is in origin an English legal term, *bordland*, meaning 'land providing supplies (board) for a (lord's) table'. It is first found in *Bracton* (c. 1225), an influential treatise on English law and custom. In England the term does not seem to have been used as a place-name, but in Scotland it eventually became established over a wide area, ranging from Inverness-shire to Galloway.

The explanation for Pont's *Boirland of Kingston* is probably to be found in a series of charters. By *RMS* ii, 2520, already referred to, the king, James IV, confirmed Patrick Clugston of that Ilk in the possession of lands which included **Boreland**, Kirkcowan. By *RMS* ii, 2578, Patrick sold and alienated the lands to John Dunbar of Mochrum, under service of ward to the king. On 29 January 1508 (*RMS* ii, 3294) the king conceded to Patrick, son of John Dunbar, the lands of **Clugston** (354574, Kirkcowan, habitation) in a free barony. The lands had been held by service of ward and relief, but because Patrick Clugston had alienated the greater part of them without royal consent, they were first returned to the king, who then bestowed them on Patrick Dunbar in free barony, with rights of jurisdiction from his *caput* at Clugston. Pont's *Kingston* thus refers to the *caput*, Clugston, and indicates the king's ultimate authority over it. The board supplied by this Boreland was for Clugston, or for Clugston and the manor of **Gass** (335578, Kirkcowan, habitation), which formed part of the estate.

The name Boreland does not appear in the third charter mentioned, but possibly *Brandland*, in 'the 4 merkland of Brandland', may be a scribal error for Bordland, itself a 4 merkland.

Maidland, 431546, Wigtown, habitation; Pont, *Maidland*: Maxwell remarks: 'Made land, i.e. land that has been made. Much of this farm consists of land reclaimed by embanking the estuary of the river Bladnoch'.

Bruntland Plantation, 366443, Mochrum: 'burnt land' – 'rough, mossy ground, formerly burnt over periodically' (*SND*). The burning cleared the land for cultivation and pasture.

(c) Names in *-park*, 'a piece of land enclosed for a particular purpose ... a meadow or pasturage; a field (?chiefly or only, for grazing)' (*DOST*)

Mulloch Park, 295693, Penninghame, habitation: see above, chapter 5 (i).

Blackpark, 382646, Penninghame, habitation: 'black' refers to the colour of the soil.

Wellpark Burn, 307637-329628, Kirkcowan: *Well* (*wall*) in Scots means 'a natural spring of water which forms a pool or stream' (*SND*). The stream took its name from the 'park' or meadow through which it flowed.

Yettown Park, 475491, Sorbie, habitation: see above, chapter 2.

Reiffer Park, 444453, Sorbie, habitation: 'enclosure where reivers held their stolen cattle' ('*Refar*: a robber; a raider or marauder; a plunderer' *DOST*).

Moss Park, 411435, Glasserton, habitation: 'enclosure in a moss [Ravenstone Moss]'

Marlepark Cottage, 423431, Whithorn, habitation: 'enclosure where marl is dug up'. Marl was used as a fertilizer. Cf. **Marl Hole**, 350454, Mochrum.

Common Park, 451408, Whithorn, habitation: 'common pasturage (for animals belonging to the burgesses of Whithorn)'.

Broompark, 438401, Whithorn, habitation: 'field where broom grows'.

Mochrum Park, 362572, Wigtown, habitation, shows a different, and later, use of 'park'. Here it means 'a large ornamental piece of ground ... attached to or surrounding a country house or mansion ... in this sense often forming part of the name of a country house or mansion' (*OED*). In 1859 Sir William Dunbar, 7th baronet of Mochrum (1812-89), railway magnate, MP and later a senior Civil Servant, purchased the **Grange of Bladnoch** and **Torhouskie** estates in Wigtown parish, on which he built a house. House and lands were renamed Mochrum Park, commemorating the ancestral estates which had been dispersed before his time.

For something of the earlier history of the Dunbar family see above **Boreland**, 352583, Kirkcowan, habitation. The baronetcy was created in 1694.

Other examples of 'Park' in this latter sense are to be found in

Sheep Park, 390514, Kirkinner, habitation, and **Barnbarroch Park**, 4051, Kirkinner, field name. These originally belonged to the park of **Barnbarroch House**, 399515, home of the Vans Agnews; the sheep in Sheep Park had an ornamental as well as an agricultural function. Cf. **Horse Park Plantation**, 4138, Glasserton, and **Shrubbery Park**, 4237, Glasserton, both originally parts of the grounds of the lost ***Glasserton House***. The extensive grounds, which reached as far as **New England Plantation**, 437396, Glasserton, are clearly marked on Ainslie's map of 1782, at which time they belonged to the Honourable Admiral Keith Stewart.

(d) Miscellaneous names associated with human habitation or occupation

Wells of the Rees, 229723, Kirkcowan, habitation: 'so named because of their proximity to sheep *rees*' [*ree*, 'permanent stone sheepfold'] 'said to have been built from the fabric of the old church' [**Kilgallioch**, 229723, Kirkcowan]. '(They) are three springs covered by domed structures of large unmortared stones ... They are traditionally said to have been resorted to by penitents for religious ceremonies etc.' (*RCAHMS, Canmore*).

Knowe, 311713, Penninghame, habitation: Scots *know*, 'hillock, knoll'. The word was sometimes applied to a supposed fairy-mound.

Closes, 324685, Penninghame, habitation: plural of *close*, 'enclosure, courtyard'. The name probably means 'enclosures'.

Kiln Fauld, 259666, Kirkcowan, habitation: 'an enclosed piece of ground (*fauld*) with a kiln (for parching corn before grinding)'. 'The primitive stone-built corn kiln' survived 'until at least the 1850s ... in isolated upland districts' (Donnachie 1971, 31).

Blackquarter, 360661, Penninghame, habitation: 'black locality'. The probable meaning of *-quarter* is 'one of the areas (probably originally a fourth part) into which a parish was divided for the purposes of poor relief and the distribution of elders' duties; more generally a locality, district' (*SND*). *Black-* may refer to the colour of the soil, or indicate that the poor of the area were in unusually bad condition. The name is post-Reformation and has nothing to do with the quarterlands of early Gaelic society.

Hazlie Green, 387644, Penninghame, habitation: ‘green with hazels growing on it’.

Carty Port, 432625, Penninghame; **Carty Bridge** (over an unnamed tributary of the Cree), 432624, habitation: **Carty Farm**, 428627, habitation: obscure. Only *Carty Port* figures on Ainslie’s map (1782); the other names, it would seem, derive from this. *Port* implies that shipping berthed here, also, probably, that it was the site of a ferry across the Cree, possibly a ferry capable of taking carts?

Kelly Port, 446612, Penninghame: site of another minor port, probably operated by someone called Kelly. At the site, which does not figure on Ainslie’s map, there is a disused quay.

Liggat Check Cottage, 422610, Penninghame, habitation; Ainslie 1782, *Clary Legget*: *liggat* is ‘a self-closing gate’; *check* probably indicates that passing travellers were checked, and paid the appropriate toll, at this gate. The cottage is on the A714, half-a-mile north of **Causeway End**, 421600, Penninghame, habitation. The causeway which preceded the A714 was presumably across **Carse of Clary**. There is also a **Causeway End Wood**, 4260, and a **Causeway End Bridge** (across the **Bishop Burn**), 421594. See also **Red Legget**, 407507, Kirkinner. Ainslie also marks ***Near Legget***, ***Mid Legget*** and ***Fare Legget*** on the partially completed road from Whithorn to Port William (now the B7021) and ***Leggatcheck*** at Castlewigg, on what is now the A746. Pennyliggit, 118591, Inch, habitation, is on the A75, east of Castle Kennedy.

Balgreen, 329603, Kirkcowan, habitation: the *ba’green*, the grassy field on which the people of Kirkcowan once played football.

Loudon Hill, 419602, Penninghame, habitation: probably not a hill-name, but a commemoration of the success gained by the Covenanters against Claverhouse in the skirmish (1679) at Drumclog under Loudoun Hill in Avondale parish, Lanarkshire.

Grange of Cree, 454594, Penninghame, habitation; **Grange of Bladnoch**, 365575, Wigtown, habitation; Pont, *Grainge*: ‘Grange’ is ‘an outlying farm with barns etc. belonging to a religious establishment or a feudal lord, where crops and tithes in kind were stored’ (*OED*). Possibly both belonged originally to the priory of Whithorn. It is worth noting that Thomas Randolph, 1st earl of Moray (c.1275-1332) granted all his fishery in the Cree to the priory (*RMS* i, Appendix 1, 20, 20 May 1325). The activities at Grange of Cree may once have been directed towards the drying, smoking and salting of fish stocks and the maintenance of stanks and fishponds; see Oram 2005, under the heading *Fisheries*.

Spittal, 360578, Wigtown, habitation: *spital*, 'a place built by ancient charity, as of the Church, the Knights Hospitallers, etc., for the accommodation of the sick or the destitute, later specifically in Scotland, a hospice or shelter, especially in mountainous country, for travellers. Frequent in place-names throughout Scotland' (*SND*).

Situated as it is, under **Boat Hill**, 362577, at the crossing of the Bladnoch (now **Spitta**l **Bridge**) on the B733, linking Kirkcowan and points west with Wigtown and Whithorn, this particular *spital* appears to have been built primarily for pilgrims coming from the west to Whithorn; see MacQueen 2002, 21.

Borrow Moss, 4357, Wigtown; **Borrowmoss**, 435570, habitation; Pont *Burrowmoss*, habitation; **Borrowmoss Bridge** (over **Borrowmoss Burn**), 434569: *burgh moss*, the bog on which the burgesses of the royal burgh of Wigtown grazed their cattle and from which they dug peat for fuel.

Newmilns, 403553, Wigtown, habitation; Pont, *Newmyll*: 'new (corn-)mill', powered by the water of the neighbouring burn. The mill must have been built at latest in the 16th century.

Killiebrakes, 311525, Mochrum, 77 m.: see above, chapter 4 (b).

Braehead, 420522, Kirkinner, habitation: self-explanatory. On Ainslie's 1782 map it is called ***Newtown***.

Jacob's Ladder, 370516, Kirkinner: the reference, apparently, is to Jacob's dream in Genesis 28, 11-19. The relevance is unclear.

Red Legget, 407507, Kirkinner, habitation: see above, **Liggat Check Cottage**, 422610. Red Legget is a cottage on the A714, linking **Wigtown** and **Port William**. It too may once have serviced a toll-gate, presumably one painted red.

March Farm, 399492, Kirkinner, habitation; **March Farm Row**, 398492: 'farm on the *march* or boundary', perhaps the boundary of the pre-Reformation parish of Longcastle; *row* or *raw* is 'a row of houses ... especially applied to the cottages of miners or farm-servants' (*SND*).

Stonehouse, 412473, Sorbie, habitation (not recorded by Pont, but on Ainslie's 1782 map): a stone-built farmhouse, unlike the clay-and-wattle buildings which had been usual before. It was presumably the first stone farmhouse in the district.

Moormains, 351445, Mochrum, habitation; **Moormains Bridge** (over the **Killantrae Burn**), 349445: 'Mains on the moor'. For *Mains*, 'the house farm of an estate, cultivated by or for the proprietor', see MacQueen 2002, 19-20. The estate was probably that of the Maxwells of Monreith.

Bridgehouse (Brighouse), 431443, Whithorn, habitation: 'house at a bridge', now **Drummond Hill Bridge**, 431442, on the A746, across a small stream. Once a toll-house?

Port William, 338437, Mochrum, habitation: 'Sir William Maxwell of Monreith founded and gave his name to this small port village c. 1776' (Donnachie 1971, 239).

Culloden Plantation, 4242, Whithorn: so named to commemorate the battle fought in 1746 between Jacobites and Hanoverians. It is not marked on Ainslie's 1782 map and is probably a product of the romanticism inspired by Sir Walter Scott's poems and novels.

Mains, as in **High Mains**, 445395, Whithorn, habitation; **Low Mains**, 447391, habitation; **Low Mains Cottage**, 446390, habitation; *RMS* iv, 2823, 1 January 1579, *Manys de Quhithorne*; Pont, *Mains*; **Mains Loch**, 452388: 'house-farm (of the Priory of Whithorn)'.

(e) *Hole*, 'small bay'; *Isle*, 'rock near the shore'; see MacQueen 2002, 5, 28. Most of these names are self-explanatory.

Begg's Hole, 492483, Sorbie: Begg, Gaelic *beag*, 'small', is a common surname.

Brown's Hole, 494467, Sorbie.

Bottle Hole Bridge (on the A747, just north of Port William), 338442, Mochrum: obscure.

Howe Hole of Shaddock, 477396, Whithorn: *howe* means 'hollow, lying in a hollow, deep-set, sunken'. *Shaddock* is **Sheddock**,

472395, Whithorn, the farm bordered to the east by the little bay.

Blockan Hole, 440345, Whithorn: 'little bay where young coalfish (*blockan*) are caught'.

Thief's Hole, 464334, Whithorn: in Scots, *thief's hole* means 'cell, dungeon'. The reference here is to the steepness of the cliffs which partly encircle the little bay.

Jamie's Hole, 463343, Whithorn.

A different, probably later, usage is found in **Marl Hole**, 350454, Mochrum. *Hole* here means the pit from which marl, used as a fertilizer, was extracted.

Isles of Burrow, 461341, Whithorn: 'rocks near the shore at **Burrow Head** (457430, Whithorn)'.

In **Isle of Whithorn**, 4736, Whithorn, habitation (*RMS* i, Appendix 1, 20, 20 May 1325, *Port Witerne*; ii, 383, 10 August 1450, *Portquihitherne*; 453, 20 June 1451, *Insule de Porthquhitirn*; 461, 1 July 1451, *Port Wyterne*; iv, 2823, 1 January 1579, *Insula de Quhithorne*; Pont, *Yll of Whitorn*) the usage is different and closer to English. The original name appears to have been ***Isle of Port Whithorn***, with 'Isle' referring to the formerly tidal island on the east side of **Isle of Whithorn Bay**, on the beaches of which travellers and pilgrims would land at low tide. The bay was the port-of-entry for sea-traffic to Whithorn.

For the possibility that the original name of the village was Bysbie, see above, chapter 7.

A few other coastal names deserve mention. **Rigg Bay**, 4744, Sorbie, is 'ridge bay', referring to the ridges of rock across the bay. In **Sliddery Point**, 486441, Sorbie, the first element means 'slippery'. 'Ducker', in **Ducker Craig**, 438436, Whithorn, and **Ducker Rock**, 450340, Whithorn, means 'a diving bird', such as the shag (*scart*) or the cormorant. 'Port', as in **Port Allen**, 478410, Sorbie, or **White Port**, 479404, Whithorn, generally indicates a place where it was possible to bring a small boat to land.

Looking north from Cruggleton Castle; Sliddery Point, Eggerness Point, and the southern part of the 'boundary ridge'.

(f) Stream-names

Gaelic stream-names have already been discussed; here I shall only mention some typical Scots names. *Water*, as in Tarf Water or Water of Malzie, usually implies a stream of some size. The usual word for smaller streams is *burn*. *Strand* and *lane* occur infrequently. **Lane Burn** is a tautology; the stream is formed by the junction of the Mildriggan and Kirkland Burns, and enters the Bladnoch at 438541, above Wigtown Harbour.

Some stream-names are descriptive. The **Black Burn**, which has a long and winding moorland course before its junction with the Bladnoch at 338659, takes its name from its dark peaty water. The **Brushy Burn**, which joins the Cree below **Brushy Bridge**, 434622, Penninghame, takes its name from the brush, thick undergrowth, which grows, or once grew, beside it. The name **Ket Water**, a stream which flows through Whithorn to enter Wigtown Bay at Portyerrock, 477388, Whithorn, habitation, is similar; it is derived from the vegetation or type of soil along its course; *ket* is 'couch-grass' or 'a spongy kind of peat composed of tough matted fibres' (*SND*).

For the most part, however, streams take their names from the places they pass, for instance, **Beoch Burn** (**Beoch**, 321717, Penninghame, habitation), **Barhoise Burn** (**Barhoise Farm**, 338619, Kirkcowan, habitation), **Clugston Burn** (**Clugston**, 354574, Kirkcowan, habitation), **Killantrae Burn** (**High** and **Low Killantrae**, 328460, 331457, Mochrum, habitations), **Ersock Burn** (**High** and **Low Ersock**, 441375, 446378, Glasserton, habitations). Occasionally a name changes during the course of the stream; the **Inch Burn** (**Inch**, 447475, Sorbie, habitation) becomes the **Kilfillan Burn**. ***Kilfillan*** is recorded as a habitation by Pont and Ainslie, but has since disappeared.

Occasionally the stream takes its name from a notable local feature. **Ha' Hill Strand**, for instance, takes its name from the neighbouring **Ha' Hill**, 229704, 196 m.. The **Maltkiln Burn** is probably named from a kiln producing malt for Mildriggan Mill, 421521, Kirkinner, mentioned in chapter 2.

Streams often marked boundaries, and this is sometimes

commemorated in the name. **March Burn**, for instance, marked the boundary between the lands of Eldrig (High and Low Eldrig, 249691, 251679, Kirkcowan, habitations) and Dirneark, 262704, Kirkcowan, habitation. **Bishop Burn**, which enters the Cree at 459586, separated land held by the Bishop of Whithorn, primarily from that held by the burgesses of Wigtown.

Eighteenth-century and subsequent innovations in field-drainage have affected the course and the volume of water in most streams. The name and the unusually straight course of **The Canal**, 393496-396504, indicate that it is a product of the Improvements. **The Black Ditch**, 443496-446446, Whithorn, is another product of a new drainage system.

There are two names which I cannot explain. **Stirnie Birnie Burn** runs under **Stirnie Birnie Bridge**, 448412, Whithorn (on the B7004), to enter Ket Water below Claywhippart Bridge, 455404. The name may be a nonsense formation. **Mother Water** issues from Mains Loch, 452388, Whithorn, to join the Ersock Burn at 447378.

(g) Names of woods

Names in Gaelic *doire*, 'oak-wood', were discussed in chapter 6. These may be ancient. Names discussed here are more recent – as a consequence of the work of the Forestry Commission, some even very recent. The common element *Plantation* (*Plantin'*) generally indicates a wood or grove planted during the Improvements either as a wind-break or, on an estate, for ornamental purposes. Possibly earlier Scots names are few.

Fiddle Wood, 372684, Penninghame: uncertain; it is close to the ruins of the seventeenth-century **Castle Stewart**, 379689, Penninghame, habitation, (now Pennighame House), and may have belonged to the fiddler who provided music for the castle. Alternatively, wood suited for the making of fiddles may have been found there. The word 'fiddle' is found in Scots from the late fifteenth century; the instrument has been around for at least as long. Most were made locally.

Shank Wood, 314624, Kirkcowan: *Shank* sometimes means 'a downward spur or projection of a hill' (*SND*). This corresponds to the position of the wood on a gentle hill-slope above the **Wellpark Burn**.

Old Lands Wood, 393520, Kirkinner: see above, **Oldland**, 321611, Kirkcowan, habitation.

Shabby Braes Wood, 467440, Sorbie, habitation: *Shabby* probably has the obsolete sense, 'dirty, muddy'. The *braes* are the hill-slopes above the **Broughton Burn**. The wood has disappeared.

Fey Wood, 405438, Glasserton: *Fey* means 'infield or cultivated land nearest the farm-buildings in the old system of tillage' (*SND*). The fermtoun in question was probably that of **Ravenstone Castle**, 409441, Glasserton, habitation. The wood would have been planted only after the fey and the fermtoun had disappeared in the course of the eighteenth-century Agricultural Revolution.

(h) Hill-names

Hill-names often consist simply of the name of a nearby habitation, usually a farm, followed by the word 'hill' or 'fell'. Many of these have already been listed under the habitation-name. Most of these now listed have a more descriptive kind of first element.

The Stand, 257741, Kirkcowan, 190 m.: *Stand* here means 'station, stance', perhaps in the sense 'the standing place from which a hunter or sportsman may shoot game' (*OED*). Compare Knocknassie, NW 979687, Kirkcolm, 87 m.: *cnoc an fhasaidh*, 'hill of the stance'.

Bught Hill, 221727, Kirkcowan, 212 m.: *Bught*, *bucht*, or *bowcht* is a sheepfold, in particular 'a milking fold for ewes' (*DOST*).

Ha' Hill, 229705, Kirkcowan, 196 m.: is probably 'hawthorn hill'. Cf. **Haw Hill**, 315636, below.

Green Knowe, 313655, Kirkcowan, 182 m., is the northernmost summit in a ridge of hills which includes **Shennock Fell**, 313652, 192 m., **Culvennan Fell**, 311650, 213 m., and **Fell End**, 307643, Kirkcowan, 201 m. *Knowe* means 'hillock'; *Fell* is derived from Old Norse *fjall*, 'mountain', but was early adapted into Scots and is so to be regarded here. For **Shennock**, 317660, habitation, and **Culvennan**, **West**, 297651, and **East**, 307655, habitations, see above, chapter 5. *Fell* is common in hill names, generally in conjunction with some habitation name from the neighbourhood of the hill.

Fell End has the following spurs:

Rough Gibb, 303642; cf. **Rough Gib**, 402560, Wigtown, 59 m.: *gib* may be a form of Scots *kip*, 'a jutting or projecting point on a hill' (*SND*). There is also a **Loch Gib**, 397560, Wigtown.

High Wether Layers, 311642. *Wether* is a castrated ram; *layer* is Scots *lair*, 'a place where animals lie down, a fold or enclosure for cattle or sheep' (*SND*).

Bennylow, 303641. See above, chapter 5.

Bizziard Fell, 304639: 'buzzard fell'.

Gallows Hill, 387638, Penninghame, 57 m.; 308502, Mochrum, 150 m.; 467357, Whithorn: self-explanatory; cf. **Gallow Hill**, 469434, below. The respective jurisdictions involved were probably those of Merton Hall, 382639, of Old Place of Mochrum, 307541, and of the Bishop, or the Prior of Whithorn. The plural form *gallows* indicates that these names are later than that of Gallow Hill, with the singular.

Haw Hill, 315636, Kirkcowan, 107 m.: 'hawthorn hill'.

Kiln Hill, 385609, Penninghame, 67 m.; 376554, Kirkinner, 43 m.; 452466, Sorbie, 38 m.: 'hill with a kiln on it'. The reference is probably to corn-kilns, built on hills for the augmented draught.

Molland Hill, 386593, Wigtown, 81 m.; Pont, *Drummollyinhill*, habitation; **Little Molland**, 386599, 69 m.: *druim muilinn*, 'mill ridge'. Cf. above chapter 5.

Nuttree Hill, 356592, Wigtown, 62 m.: self-evident.

Auld Hill, 378592, Wigtown, 89 m.: probably 'old hill'. *Auld* may, however, be *allt*, which in Irish Gaelic means 'a height, glenside', in Scottish Gaelic 'a stream'. If this is so, the reference is to the glen of the **Bartrostan Burn**, which flows under the hill on the south-west side, or to the burn itself.

Boat Hill, 353589, Kirkcowan, 37 m.: either 'hill shaped like a boat' or 'hill where there was a ferry-boat across the Bladnoch'.

Gorty Hill, 349577, Kirkcowan, 66 m.: obscure.

Boat Hill, 362576, Wigtown, 42 m.: see above. This hill stands above Spittal Bridge across the Bladnoch, probably once the site of a ferry for pilgrims and others on the road from the west to Whithorn.

Gool Hill, 361575, Wigtown, 42 m.: *Gool* is probably Scots *gowl*, *goule*, *gool*, 'a deep hollow between hills' (*SND*), 'a narrow pass' (*DOST*). The reference is probably to the gap between Boat Hill, 362576, and Gool Hill, through which the B733 passes on its way to Wigtown and Whithorn. I can find no landscape feature to support Maxwell's suggestion that *Gool* represents Gaelic *gobhal*, 'fork'.

Strife Hill, 408573, Wigtown, 57 m.: the reference is probably to some past legal or other dispute.

Windy Hill, 430555, Wigtown, 57 m.: self-explanatory.

Milton Hill, 428523, Kirkinner, 27 m.: see above, chapter 2.

Braehead, 420522, Kirkinner, habitation: 'top of the brae or slope'. On the north slope above the Maltkiln Burn.

Shaw Hill, 355499, Mochrum, 106 m.: 'hill with a small wood, *shaw*, on it'.

Whaup Hill, 402493, Kirkinner, 73 m.; **Whauphill**, 403498, habitation: 'curlew (*whaup*) hill'.

Outtle Well, 464479, Sorbie: *Outtle* is probably 'outer hill'; the name thus means 'well on the outer hill'. The hill is 28 m. in height. What 'outer' refers to, is unclear.

Moudie Hill, 391477, Kirkinner, 76 m.: *moudie* is 'mole'. 'mole-hill' or 'hill where moles flourish'.

White Hills, 450466, Sorbie, habitation: *White* probably implies that originally the hills were fallow, used only for pasture. The reference may be to **Kiln Hill**, 452466, above, perhaps also the field name **Hillsborough**, 443464, 52 m., on the south side of the flat bog land around Inch and Sorbie. This last, however, bears some relationship to Hillsborough, 3235, Co. Down, 'a name originally given to a fortress built c. 1610 by Sir Moses Hill, Provost Marshall of Ulster, near Belfast on the Co. Antrim side of the river [Lagan]' (McKay 1999, 81). The name was later transferred to the modern site, where Government House, once the official residence of the Governor of Northern Ireland, now stands.

Calfward Hill, 452457, Sorbie, 43 m.: '*cauf-*, *calf-ward*: an enclosure for calves' (*SND*); 'hill with an enclosure for calves'.

Inshaw Hill, 450445, Whithorn, 51 m.: 'inner hill with a small wood on it' – inner, perhaps, with reference to Old Place of Broughton, 457451, now demolished.

Brownhill, 468439, Sorbie, 57 m., habitation: self-explanatory. **Shabby Braes Wood**, 467440, is on the north side of the hill.

Gallow Hill, 469434, Sorbie, 70 m.: 'hill with gallows on it', probably under the jurisdiction of Cruggleton Castle, 485429. For the singular form, see MacQueen 2002, 19.

Court Hill, 376427, Mochrum, 84 m.: 'hill where an open-air baron court was held', probably that of the Maxwells of Monreith.

Linkhall Hill, 399412, Glasserton, 72 m.: obscure.

Sour Hill, 453408, Whithorn, 48 m.: 'hill with cold, wet soil'.

Blindwalls Hill, 469402, Whithorn, 48 m.: obscure.

Backbraes, 421401, Whithorn, habitation (on hill, 107 m.): 'slopes at the back of, furthest remove from, some property (perhaps ***Glasserton House***)'.

Howe Hill of Haggagmalag, 455355, Whithorn, 60 m.: *howe* means 'hollow'. *Haggagmalag* remains obscure. It may be a nonsense-name.

Index of Place-Names in the Moors and Machars

Abbreviations and References

Aberdeen Breviary: *Breviarium Aberdonense*, 2 vols., Edinburgh, 1509-10; facsimile, 2 vols., Maitland Club: Glasgow, 1852-4.

Agnew 1864: Sir Andrew Agnew, Bt.: *The Agnews of Lochnaw: a history of the Hereditary Sheriffs of Galloway*, Edinburgh, 1864.

Ailred of Rievaux, *Life of Ninian*: Ailred of Rievaux, *Vita Niniani*, in MacQueen 2005, 102-124.

Ainslie map: *A Map of the County of Wigton or the Shire of Galloway Survey'd & Engraved By John Ainslie 1782*, Edinburgh, 1782.

Anderson 1991: Alan Orr Anderson and Marjorie Ogilvie Anderson (eds.), *Adomnán's Life of Columba,* revised by Marjorie Ogilvie Anderson, Oxford 1991.

Anglo-Saxon Chronicle: C. Plummer (ed.), *Two of the Saxon Chronicles Parallel*, Oxford, 1889.

AU: W.M. Hennessy and B. MacCarthy (eds.), *Annála Ulaidh: Annals of Ulster*, 4 vols., Dublin, 1887-1901. – Seán Mac Airt and Gearóid Mac Niocaill (eds.), *Annals of Ulster (to A.D. 1131)*, Dublin, 1983.

Barrow 1973: G.W.S. Barrow, *Kingdom of the Scots*, London, 1973.

Battle of Brunnanburh, *Battle of Maldon*: I have used the texts in A.J. Wyatt (ed.), *Anglo-Saxon Reader*, Cambridge, 1930. Translations in R.K. Gordon, *Anglo-Saxon Poetry*, London, 1954, 327-34.

Bede: B. Colgrave and R.A.B. Mynors (eds.), *Bede's Ecclesiastical History of the English People*, Oxford, 1969. Translation by Leo Sherley-Price, revised by R.E. Latham, Harmondsworth, 1968 and subsequent reprints.

Black 1946: George F. Black, *Surnames of Scotland: Their Origin, Meaning and History*, New York, 1946.

Blaeu *Atlas of Scotland,* Edinburgh, 2006.

Bracton: F.W. Maitland (ed.), *Bracton's Note Book*, London, 1887.

Breeze 2001: Andrew Breeze, 'Brittonic Place-Names from South-West Scotland, Part 2', *TDGNHAS* 75 (2001), 151-8.

Clancy 1995: T.O. Clancy, 'Annat in Scotland and the origins of the

parish', *Innes Review* XLVI, No. 2 (1995), 91-115.
Cormack 1995: W.F. Cormack, 'Excavation of a Forgotten Church Site in Galloway', *TDGNHAS* 70 (1995), 5-106.
Cowan 1967: Ian B. Cowan, *Parishes of Medieval Scotland*, Scottish Record Society: Edinburgh, 1967.

Dinneen: Patrick S. Dinneen, *Foclóir Gaedhilge agus Béarla, an Irish-English Dictionary*, Dublin, 1927.
Donnachie 1971: Ian Donnachie, *Industrial Archaeology of Galloway*, Newton Abbot, 1971.
DOST: *Dictionary of the Older Scottish Tongue*, Chicago, Aberdeen, Oxford, 1937-2002.
Dryburgh Liber: *Liber S. Marie de Dryburgh*, Bannatyne Club: Edinburgh, 1847.
DIL: E.G. Quin (ed.), *Dictionary of the Irish Language Based Mainly on Old and Middle Irish Materials*, Compact Edition, Royal Irish Academy: Dublin, 1990.
Dwelly: Edward Dwelly, *Illustrated Gaelic-English Dictionary*, Glasgow, 1901-11 and subsequent editions.

Ekwall: E. Ekwall, *Oxford Dictionary of English Place-Names*, Oxford, 1935 and subsequent editions.

GPC: *Geiriadur Prifysgol Cymru: A Dictionary of the Welsh Language*, Cardiff, 1950-. Gregory Smith 1902: G. Gregory Smith, *Specimens of Middle Scots*, Edinburgh and London, 1902.

HDGP: *Historical Dictionary of Gaelic Placenames*, Dublin, 2003-. Heist 1965: W.W. Heist (ed.), *Vitae Sanctorum Hiberniae ex Codice olim Salmanticensi nunc Bruxellensi*, *Subsidia Hagiographica*, No 28, Socièté des Bollandistes, Bruxelles, 1965.
Hill 1997: Peter Hill, *Whithorn and St Ninian: The Excavation of a Monastic Town 1984-91*, Stroud, 1995.
Hogan 1910: *Onomasticon Goedelicum Locorum et Tribuum Hiberniae et Scotiae*, Dublin and London, 1910; reprint, Dublin, 1993.

Hughes and Hannan 1992: A.J. Hughes and R.J. Hannan, *Place-Names of Northern Ireland, Volume Two; County Down II; The Ards*, Belfast 1992.

Inq. ad Cap.: T. Thomson (ed.), *Inquisitionum ad Capellam Domini Regis Retornatarum, quae in publicis archivis Scotiae adhuc servantur, Abbreviatio*, Edinburgh, 1811-16.

Joyce 1870, 1871, 1913: P.W. Joyce, *Origin and History of Irish Names of Places*, 3 vols., Dublin, 1869-1913.

Kirkwood 2007: David Kirkwood, *Garlieston: Emergence of a Village*, Stranraer, 2007.

Kneen, 1925: J.J. Kneen, *Place-Names of the Isle of Man*, Douglas, 1925; reprint, Scolar Press, Menston, 1970.

MacDonald 1941: Angus MacDonald, *Place-Names of West Lothian*, Edinburgh and London, 1941.

Macdougall 1982: Norman Macdougall, *James III, A Political Study*, Edinburgh, 1982.

MacKie 1975: Euan W. MacKie, *Scotland: An Archaeological Guide*, London, 1975.

McKay 1999: Patrick McKay, *Dictionary of Ulster Place-Names*, Belfast, 1999.

M'Kerlie 1906: P.H. M'Kerlie, *History of the Lands and their Owners in Galloway*, 2 vols., Paisley, 1906.

McNeill and MacQueen 1996: Peter G.B. McNeill and Hector L. MacQueen, *Atlas of Scottish History to 1707*, Edinburgh, 1996.

MacQueen 1956: John MacQueen, 'Kirk- and Kil- in Galloway Place-Names', *Archivum Linguisticum* 8.2 (1956), 135-49.

– 2002: *Place-Names in the Rhinns of Galloway and Luce Valley*, Stranraer, 2002.

– 2005: *St Nynia, with a translation of the Miracula Nynie Episcopi and the Vita Niniani by Winifred MacQueen*, Edinburgh, 2005.

Marwick 1952: Hugh Marwick, *Orkney Farm-Names*, Kirkwall, 1952.

Maxwell 1930: Sir Herbert Maxwell Bt., *Place Names of Galloway*, Glasgow, 1930.
Miracula Nynie Episcopi: translation in MacQueen 2005, 88-101.
MRPNA: *Melville Richards Place-Name Archive*, University of Wales, Bangor; www.bangor.ac.uk/amr/.
Murray 2006: Jane Murray, *Prehistoric Settlement in the Wigtownshire Moors*, Stranraer, 2006.
Myres 1986: J.N.L. Myres, *The English Settlements*, Oxford, 1986.

Nicolaisen 1965: W.F.H. Nicolaisen, 'Slew- and *sliabh*', *Scottish Studies* 9.1 (1965), 91-106. 1969: 'Scottish Place-Names 32: Gaelic *tulach* and *barr*', *Scottish Studies* 13.2 (1969), 159-66.
– 1976: *Scottish Place-Names*, London, 1976; revised edn., Edinburgh, 2001.

Ó Mainnín 1993: Mícheál B. Ó Mainnín, *Place-Names of Northern Ireland, Volume Three: County Down III; The Mournes*, Belfast, 1993.
ODS: David Hugh Farmer, *Oxford Dictionary of Saints*, 2nd edn., Oxford, New York, 1987.
OED: *New English Dictionary on Historical Principles* (later, *Oxford English Dictionary*), Oxford 1884-1928, with subsequent editions and supplements.
ODEPN: E. Ekwall (ed.), *Oxford Dictionary of English Place-Names*, Oxford, 1935 and subsequent editions.
Oram and Stell 1991: Richard D. Oram and Geoffrey P. Stell (eds. and contributors), *Galloway: Land and Lordship*, Edinburgh, 1991.
– 63-75, Edward J. Cowan, 'The Vikings in Galloway: A Review of the Evidence'.
– 77-95, Gillian Fellows-Jensen, 'Scandinavians in Dumfriesshire and Galloway: the Place-Name Evidence'.
Oram 2000: Richard Oram, *The Lordship of Galloway*, Edinburgh, 2000.
– 2005: *A Monastery and its Landscape: Whithorn and Monastic Estate management (c.1250-c. 1600)*, Whithorn, 2005.

Pont: Timothy Pont, *Gallovidiæ Pars Occidentalior in qua Vicecomitatus*

Victoniensis cum Regalitate Glenlucensi. The Sherifdome of Wigtoun wt the Regalitie of Glen-Luze both in Galloway: In Blaeu's *Atlas* v, Amsterdam, 1654, based on a survey made by Pont in the closing years of the sixteenth century.

Power 1952: Patrick Power, *Log-ainmneacha na nDéise: The Place-Names of Decies*, 2nd edn., Cork and Oxford, 1952.

Ptolemy: Claudius Ptolemaeus, *Geography*; for relevant sections see Rivet and Smith 1979, 103-47.

RCAHMS, Canmore: www.rcahms.gov.uk/search.html#canmore.

Robinson 1872: Samuel Robinson, *Reminiscences of Wigtonshire about the Close of Last Century*, Hamilton, 1872; reprint Wigtown, 1995.

RPC: J.H. Burton and others (eds.), *Register of the Privy Council of Scotland*, Edinburgh 1877-.

Rivet and Smith 1979: A.L.F. Rivet and Colin Smith, *Place-Names of Roman Britain*, London, 1979.

RMS: J.M. Thomson and others (eds.), *Registrum Magni Sigillii Regum Scottorum* (*Register of the Great Seal of the Kings of Scots*), Edinburgh, 1882-1914.

SND: *Scottish National Dictionary*, Edinburgh, 1927-76.

Scottish Gallovidian Encyclopedia: John MacTaggart, *Scottish Gallovidian Encyclopedia*, London, 1824; reprint Clunie Press, Perthshire, 1981.

Symson: Andrew Symson, *Large Description of Galloway*, National Library of Scotland, Advocates' MS 1856 (1684); printed Edinburgh, 1823.

Taylor 2002: Simon Taylor: 'The Element *sliabh* and the Rhinns of Galloway or Place-names and History: a Case Study', *History Scotland* 2.6, November/December 2002, 49-52.

– 2007: '*Sliabh* in Scottish Place-names: its Meaning and Chronology', *Journal of Scottish Name Studies* 1, 99-136.

TDGNHAS: *Transactions of the Dumfriesshire and Galloway Natural History and Antiquarian Society*, 1863-.

Thomas 1971: Charles Thomas, *Britain and Ireland in Early Christian Times, AD 400-800*, London, 1971.
Thurneysen 1946: Rudolf Thurneysen, *Grammar of Old Irish*, trs. by D.A. Binchy and Osborn Bergin, Dublin, 1946.

Watson 1926: W.J. Watson, *History of the Celtic Place-Names of Scotland*, Edinburgh, 1926; reprint with Introduction by Simon Taylor, Edinburgh, 2004.
Watt 1969: D.E.R. Watt, *Fasti Ecclesiæ Scoticanæ Medii Aevi ad annum 1638*, second draft, St Andrews, 1969.
Williams 1949: A.H. Williams, *Introduction to the History of Wales, I, Prehistoric Times to 1063 A.D.*, Cardiff, 1949.

Acknowledgements

The plates on pp. 46 and 150 appear coutesy of Dumfries and Galloway Museums Service (Stranraer Museum). The others are my own. Copyright of all photographs remains with the owner.

I am grateful to the School of Scottish Studies, Jack Hunter, Ian Taylor, the late R.C. Reid and the late Bill Gill who have on various occasions invited me to speak on Wigtownshire and Galloway place-names. Christine Wilson, Lynn Nield and the staff of Stranraer Library, John Pickin, Sam Miller and Alan MacFarlane, who made the map of the parishes, have been most helpful. My thanks to all.

Previous Trust Publications

Stranraer in World War Two	— Archie Bell
The Loss of the Princess Victoria	— Jack Hunter
The Cairnryan Military Railway *	— Bill Gill
A Peep at Stranraer's Past	— Donnie Nelson
Royal Burgh of Stranraer 1617 — 2000	— J.S. Boyd
	— Jack Hunter
	— Donnie Nelson
	— Christine Wilson
Don't Plague the Ferryman *	— Trevor Boult
Portpatrick to Donaghadee *	— Fraser G. MacHaffie
The Rhinns Forgotten Air Disaster *	— Sandy Rankin
Place-names in the Rhinns of Galloway	— Prof. John MacQueen
Auld Lang Syne in the Rhins of Galloway	— Prof. Charles McNeil
The Lost Town of Innermessan	— Jack Hunter
Every Beach a Port	— Bill McCormack
Aircrew in Wartime	— Norman Fidler
Prehistoric Settlement	— Dr. Jane Murray
in the Wigtownshire Moors	
100 Years of Stranraer Golf Club	— James Blair
	Andrew Hannay
	and James Sproule
Garlieston — Emergence of a Village	— David Kirkwood
A Flight Too Far	— Jack Hunter
The Story of Elsie MacKay of Glenapp	

* Out of Print

Stranraer and District Local History Trust
Membership 2008

Mrs Sheelagh Afia
Mr Peter Armitage
Mrs Elaine Barton
Mr Archie Bell, *Vice Chairman*
Mrs Dorothy Bell
Mr Douglas Brown
Mrs H.G. Brown
Mr David B. Cairns
Mr John Cameron
Mrs Pat Cameron
Mr John Carruth
Mrs Harriet Collins
Mrs Marion Cunningham
Mr J.P. Davis
Lord Dervaird
Mr Bill Dougan
Mr Jim Ferguson
Mr Norman Fidler
Mr C.J. Findlay
Miss Dora Gorman
Mrs Irene Grant
Mr Tom Hargreaves
Mrs A.C. Harkness
Mrs M.J. Heaney
Mr W.A. Heaney
Dr Patricia Heron
Mr Richard Holme
Mr Peter Holmes
Mr Jack Hunter
Mr David Kirkwood
Mr P.H.K. Lilley
Mr Robert Lindsay
Mrs Patricia Martin
Mrs Margaret MacArthur
Mrs Rosemary McCormack
Mr Colin McCubbin
Mrs J.C. MacDonald
Dr Christine McDowell
Mrs Irene McKie
Mrs Nancy McLucas
Prof. John MacQueen
Mrs Winifred MacQueen
Mr Harry Monteith
Mr Alasdair Morgan
Dr Jane Murray
Mrs Lynn Neild
Mr Donnie Nelson, MBE, *Chairman*
Mrs Mae Nelson
Mrs Helen Nish
Mr John Pickin
Mr Jim Pratt
Mrs Magaret Pratt
Mr Jim Rafferty
Mr Wolf Richthofen
Mrs Helen Scott
Mr J.D. Sharp
Mr P.N. Skinner
Dr E.A.W. Slater
Mrs Renee Smith
Lady Stair
Mr Bill Stanley
Mr D.J. Start
Mrs Sheila Stevenson
Mr Tom Stevenson, *Treasurer*
Mr Russell Walker
Mr Owen Watt
Mr David Williamson
Mr David Wilson
Mrs Christine Wilson, *Secretary*
Mrs Elizabeth Wilson
Mr Eric Wilson
Mr William Wilson
Stranraer & District Chamber of Commerce

Stranraer and District Local History Trust was constituted in 1998 at the instigation of Stranraer and District Chamber of Commerce.